BLUES BY THE BAR

Cool Riffs That Sound Great Over Each Portion of the Blues Progression

by Chris Hunt

ISBN 1-57560-479-5

Visit our website at www.cherrylane.com

Table of Contents

Introduction

If you are a guitarist who has learned the pentatonic scales up and down the neck but still secretly asks the question, "During a solo, how do I know what to play and when to play it?" then this book is for you. Also, let me assure you that you are not alone—many students come to me expressing this same sentiment. In fact, you should be congratulated for discovering that the blues is a language and not just a five-note scale. As any accomplished musician will tell you, learning to play the blues is a personal journey that requires equal amounts of listening, performing, and practicing. The goal of this book is to give you a running head start down that road by showing you a variety of riffs that you can put together "by the bar" to create complete blues solos.

Here's what lies ahead. First we'll review the standard 12-bar blues progression; then we'll break that progression down into its component parts and learn multiple riffs that work great over each. Finally, we'll put it all together with some examples of complete solos, followed by a section I call "Music Minus Me," in which you are the featured soloist.

About the Author

Chris Hunt is a New York City–based guitarist, composer, and producer. He has worked with Eddie Kendricks, the Average White Band, Joan Osborne, Martha Reeves, Mary Wells, Taylor Dayne, Brian Howe, Jocelyn Brown, Queen Esther Marrow, and the Harlem Gospel Singers, among others. He can be heard on many jingles including those for Cheerios, No Excuses Jeans, Sheraton Hotels, and Miller Lite. A graduate of Columbia University, Chris studied guitar and composition at the Berklee College of Music, as well as with Barry Galbraith and Joe Pass. In addition to being a performing and recording artist, Chris is a much sought after guitar teacher with over 20 years of teaching experience.

Acknowledgments

Many thanks to my friends at Cherry Lane—John, Mark, Rebecca, and Susan; to all my students, past and present, for keeping me on my toes; to Mark Epstein for the great bass vibe; and a special thanks to Elaine and Vivian.

The 12-Bar Blues Progression

The term *progression* is the key to understanding any piece of music. A good song, like a good story, takes you somewhere by creating and then releasing tension. We all know how this is done in the movies—think about the guy who suddenly stumbles into danger, spends the next hour or so figuring a way out, and then ends up sipping martinis on a beach.

In music, the creation and release of tension is accomplished through chords. In all of Western music—which includes classical, rock, and jazz—the IV chord creates tension, the V chord heightens that tension, and the I chord is the healing balm of release. When these three chords are played as you see them below, you've got "the blues"—arguably one of the most compelling forms of music.

12-bar Blues in G

Fig. 1

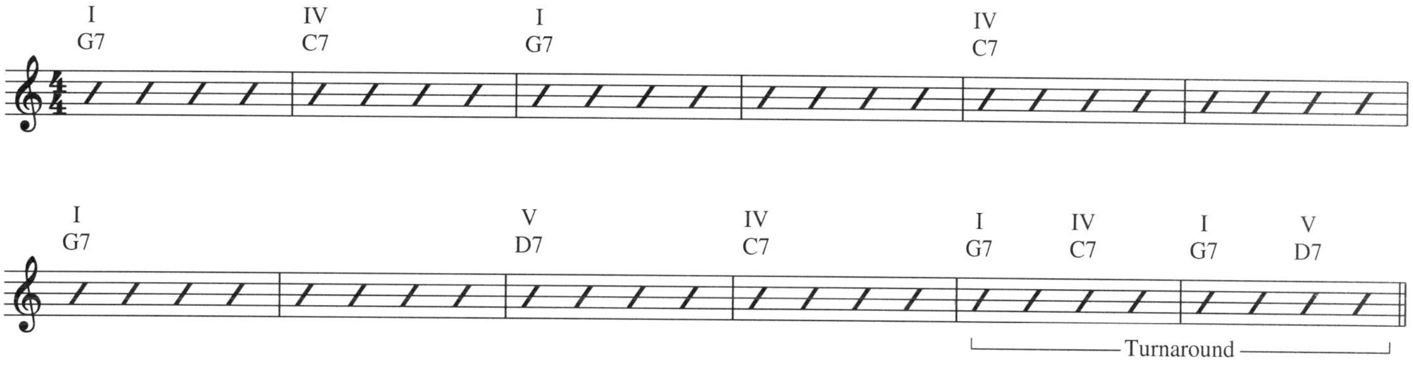

You may notice above that the "I" chord here is actually a G7 instead of just a G, the "IV" chord is actually a C7 instead of just a C, and so forth. This sort of thing is common in chord notation for the blues. Often, when players see a chord notated as just a "V," for example, they'll actually play 7ths, 9ths, 11ths, etc. along with that basic triad as well.

Because I'm the "bandleader" for this "session," I've made a few decisions. As you can see, I've chosen to play the IV chord in bar 2, when in fact many blues songs would stay on the I chord. Also, as you are probably aware, there are countless possible turnaround chord progressions (take a look at the last two bars), of which I happen to have chosen my favorite. I've included a different turnaround later on a bonus play-along track that features what's called the "slow four" so that you can hear how these riffs sound against them.

You may have noticed that I've chosen the key of G for our examples. I did this because it has been my experience that the "blues in G" is a common choice at jam sessions, and because I wanted a key that didn't allow for a good deal of open string stuff (so once you learn the riffs, you can easily move them around the neck to different keys).

Although the 12-bar form is by far the most common form of the blues, there are many ways to play it—fast, slow, with a shuffle, in a Latin style, with a swing feel, with a rock feel, in 3/4 time, etc. What all varieties of the blues share, however, is the "fire" generated by those three chords, so any of the riffs that you learn in this book will work for you in whatever blues situations you may find yourself.

Scales and Positions

Before we go any further, let's take care of some technical business. The following is a review of the fundamental scale positions for the blues. You can take a moment to look at this section now or simply refer to it later as the need arises.

In all of the examples contained in this section, the notes in parentheses are fragments of the scale (I placed them in parentheses so that you can more clearly see the full scale). If you are just starting out with scales, I recommend learning just the scale first (i.e., play only notes not in parentheses), and then adding the parenthetical notes to the fingerings.

In reality, the blues scale has six notes. In the key of G, these notes are G, B♭, C, D♭, D, and F. But, as guitar players, we play a five-note scale (the minor pentatonic scale) and call it the "blues scale" because we know that by simply bending the third note of the scale (in this case, the 3rd string at the 5th fret) up a half step, we get the pitch (here, D♭) that players of other instruments call the *blue note*. The example below includes the basic G minor pentatonic position. It can also be played up an octave at the 15th fret.

Fig. 2

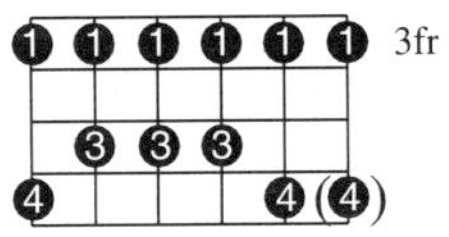

Here's a sliding position for the G minor pentatonic scale that allows one to play both below (F) and above (C) the basic position. It also allows for different hammer-on and pull-off combinations.

Fig. 3

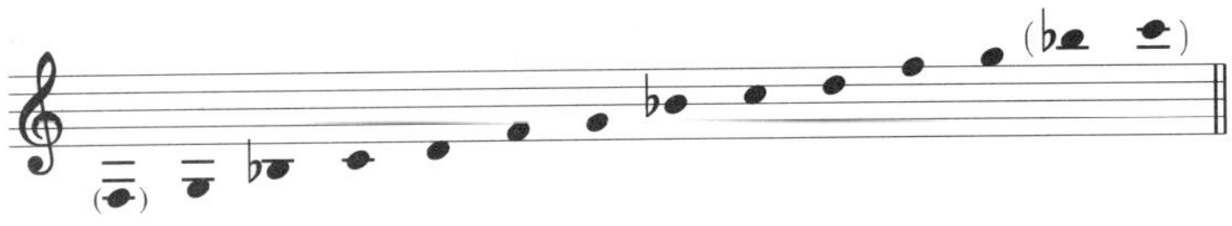

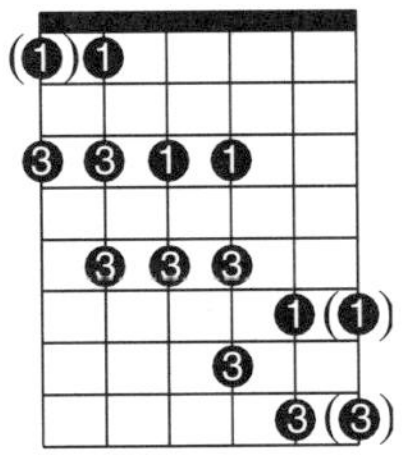

The example below shows the G minor pentatonic scale in a higher position at the 10th fret.

Fig. 4

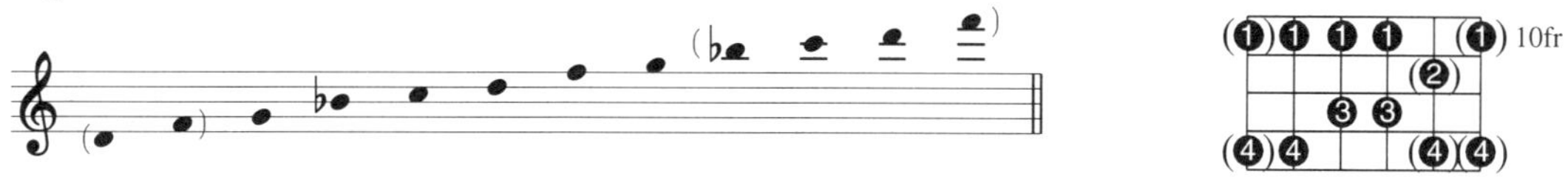

Here's another sliding position for the G minor pentatonic scale.

Fig. 5

This example shows an open position for the G minor pentatonic scale.

Fig. 6

The major pentatonic scale is also used extensively in the blues. Here's the basic G major pentatonic scale.

Fig. 7

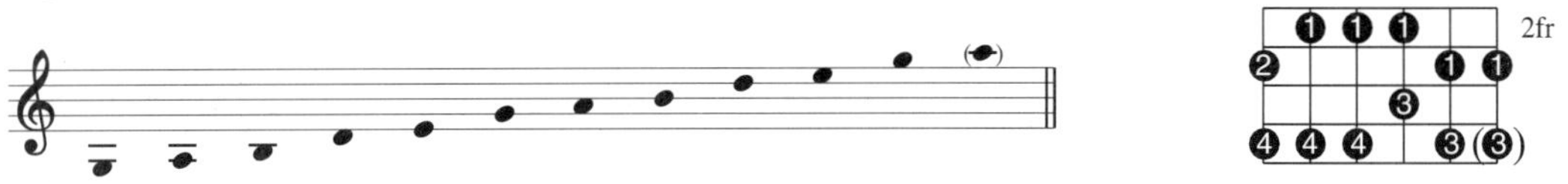

And now a sliding position for the G major pentatonic scale.

Fig. 8

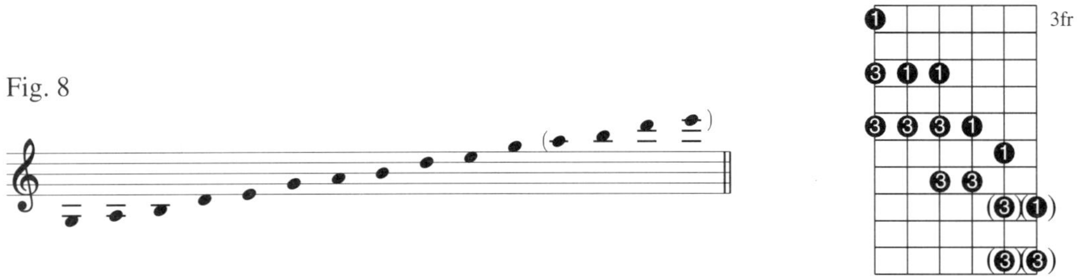

Here's a higher position for the G major pentatonic scale, with its root on the 10th fret.

Fig. 9

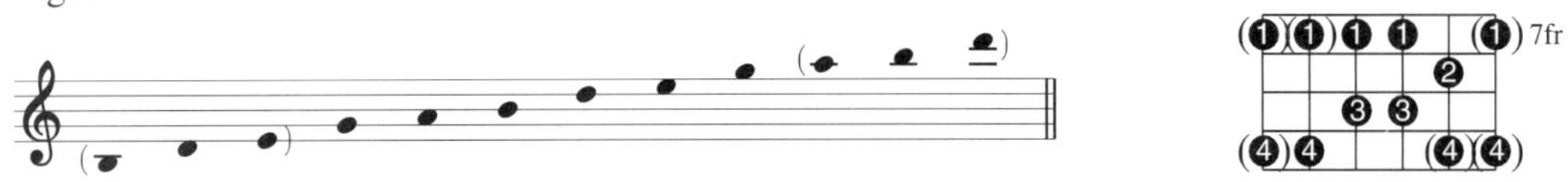

3) Talents
4) To

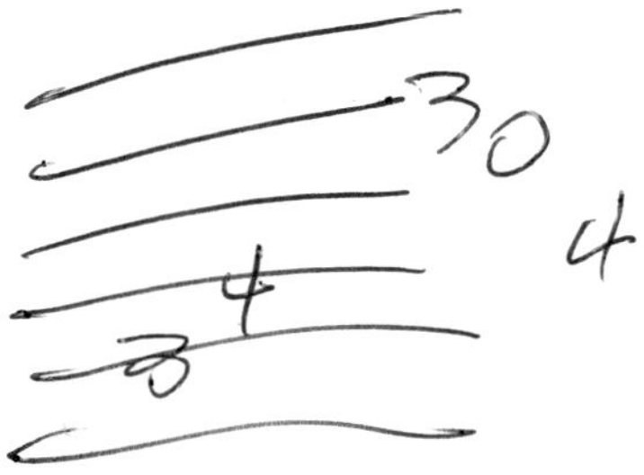

This is another position for the G major pentatonic scale, again starting at the 10th fret.

Fig. 10

And here's another sliding position for the G major pentatonic scale.

Fig. 11

Finally, here's the open position for the G major pentatonic scale.

Fig. 12

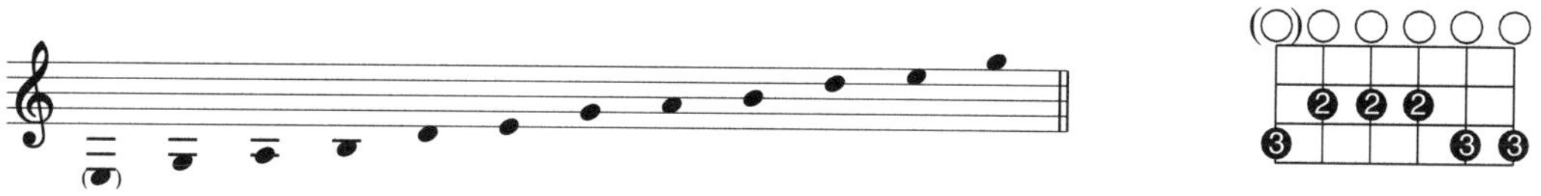

Bars 1 and 2

Let's look at the first two bars of the blues. The thing to keep in mind here is whether you are beginning a solo or are in a new cycle. If you're starting your solo, you probably want a riff that is relatively low in energy so you have someplace from which to build (Examples 1, 2, and 7). If you are in a new cycle, you might want to play a higher energy riff (Examples 8 and 10).

TRACK 1

Example 1

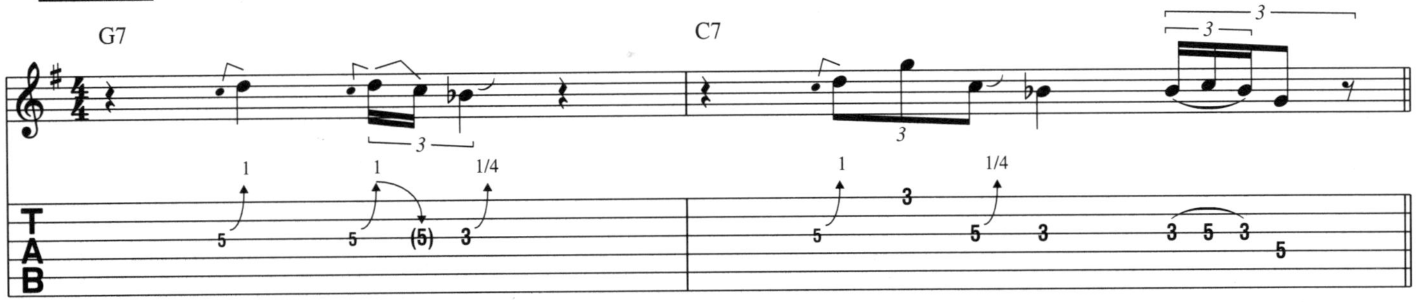

TRACK 2

Example 2

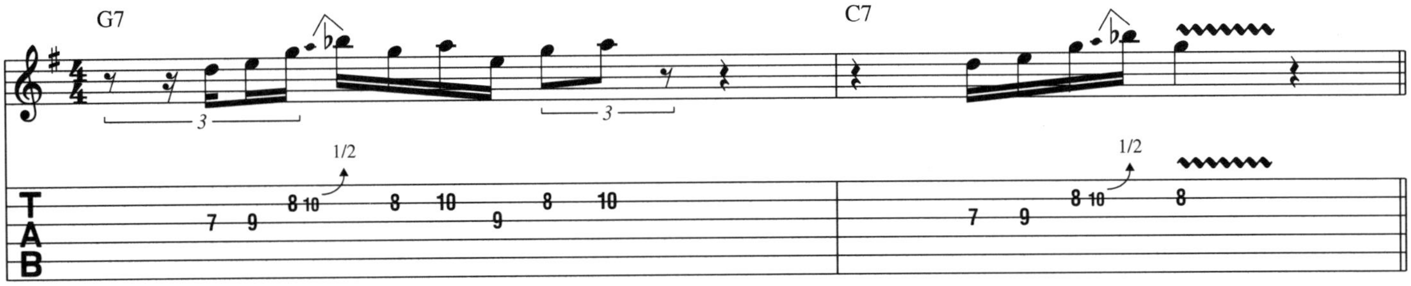

TRACK 3

Example 3

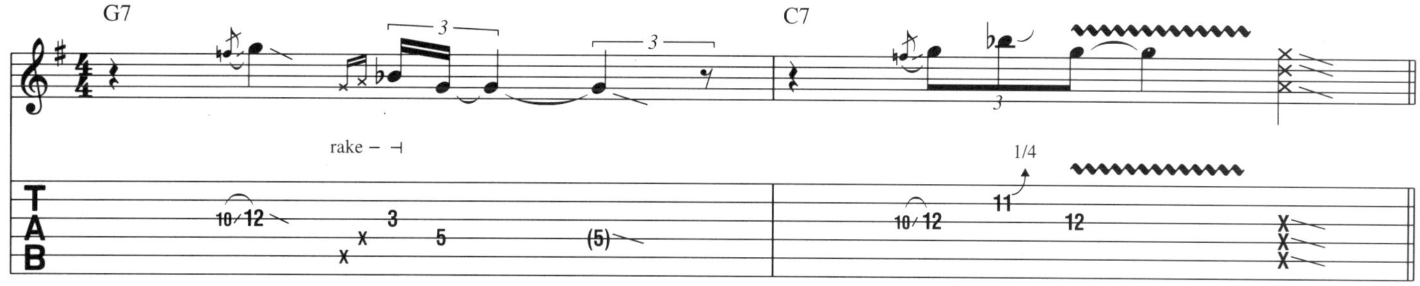

TRACK 4

Example 4

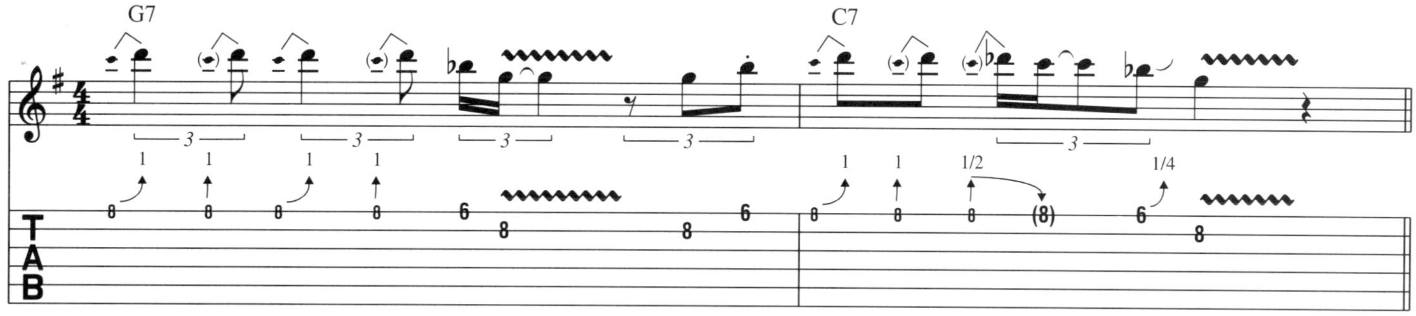

TRACK 5

Example 5

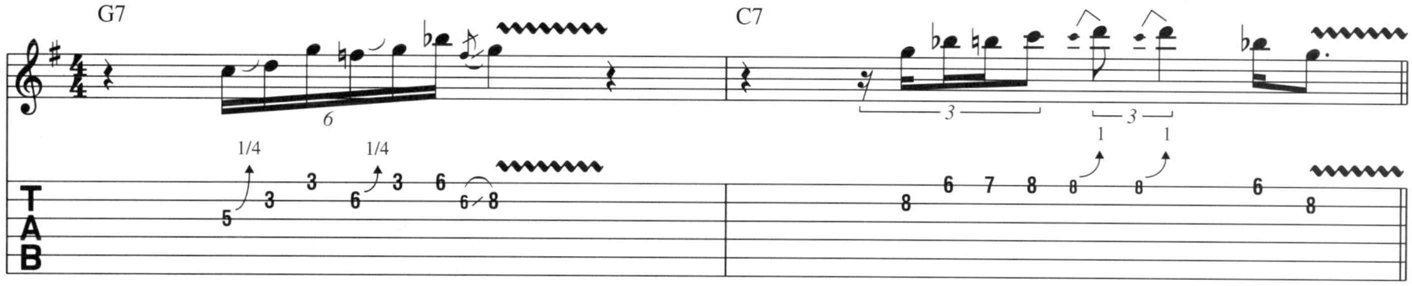

TRACK 6

Example 6

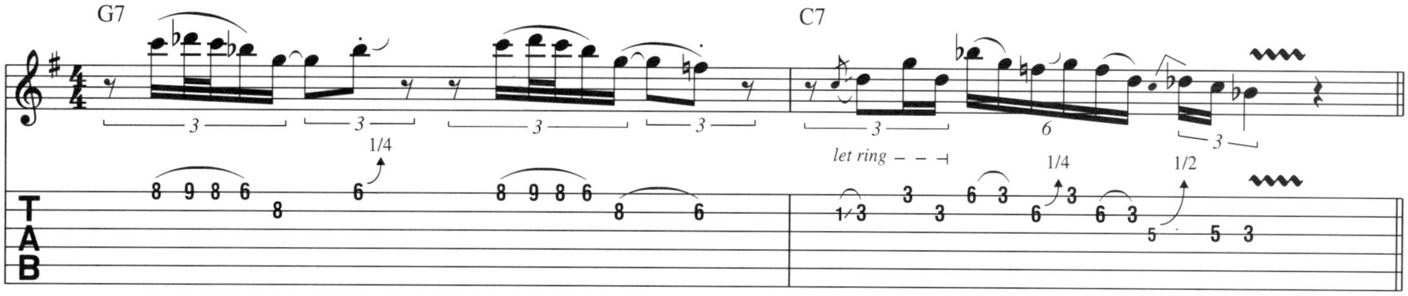

TRACK 7

Example 7

TRACK 8

Example 8

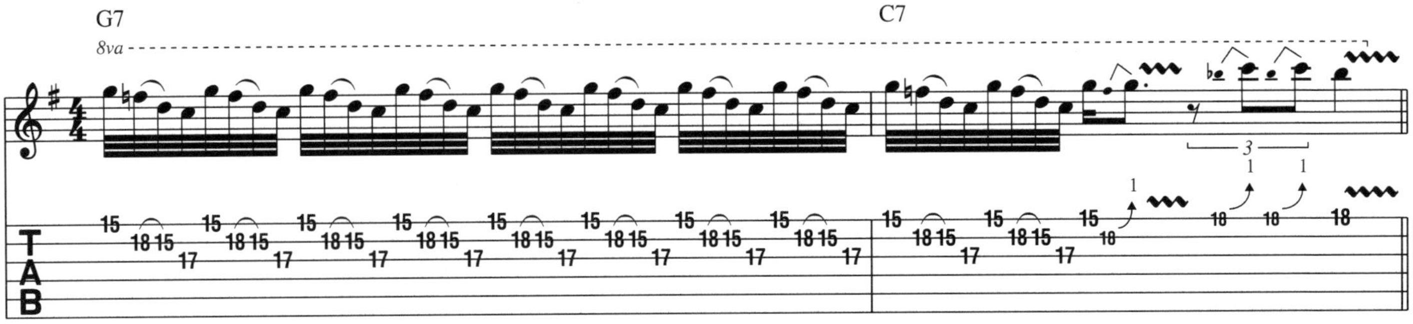

TRACK 9

Example 9

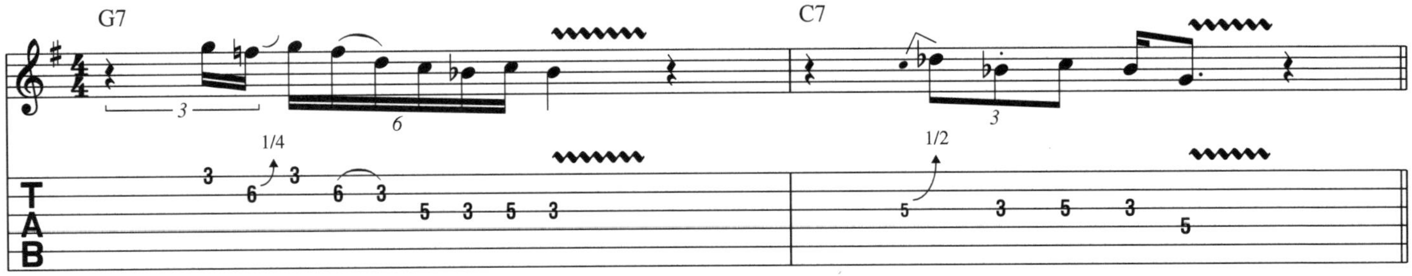

TRACK 10

Example 10

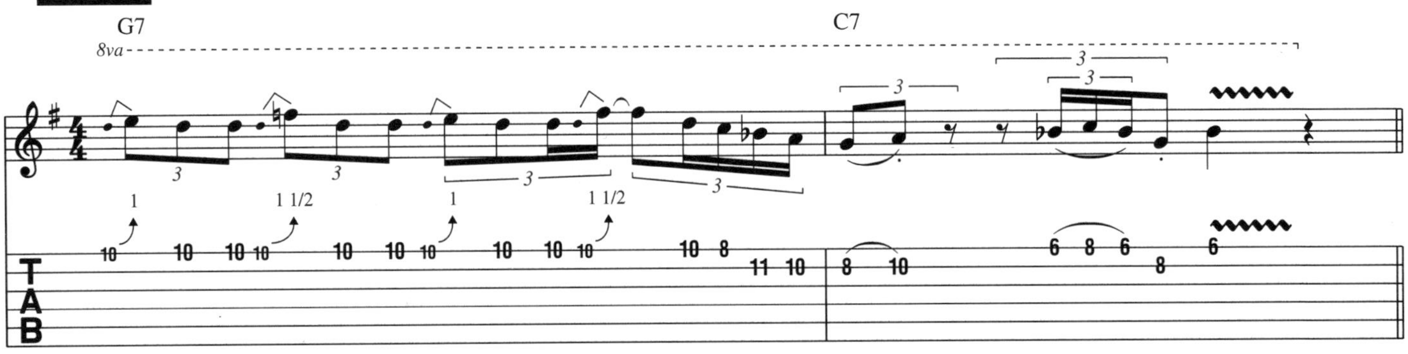

As I mentioned earlier, sometimes the blues progression goes to the IV chord in bar 2, and sometimes it remains on the I chord. While all of the above licks work in either context, here are some that really only work with one or the other. The reason for this is that these riffs use chord tones to define the harmony.

Riffs that Work with the "Fast IV"

TRACK 11

Example 11

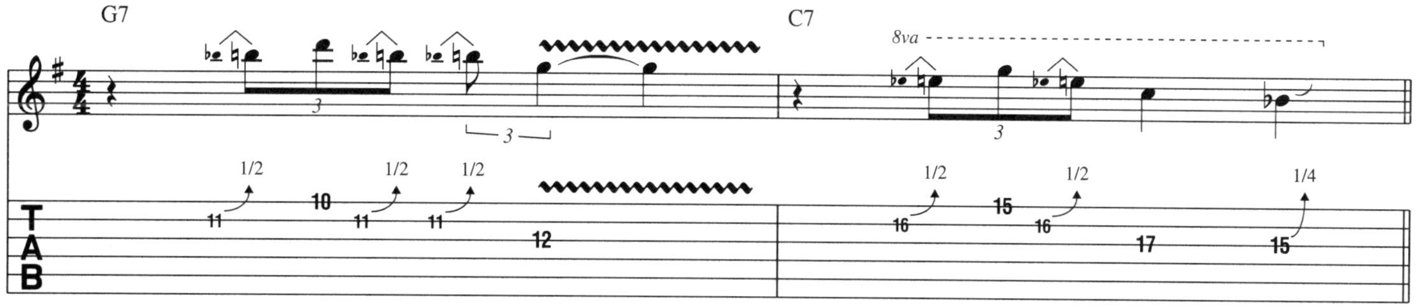

TRACK 12

Example 12

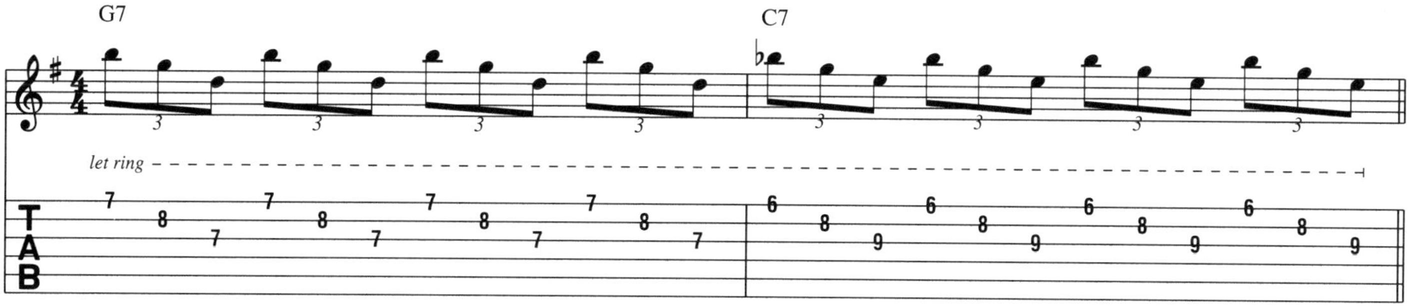

TRACK 13

Example 13

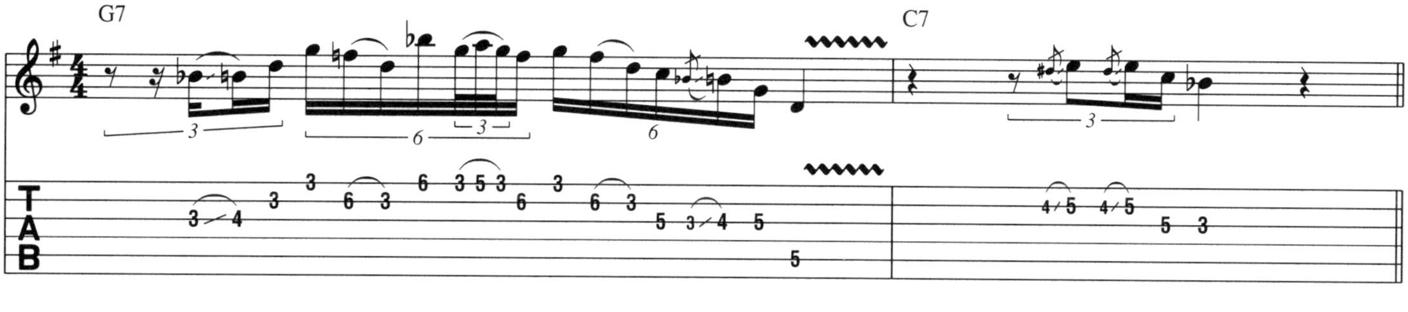

Riffs that Work with the "Slow IV"

TRACK 14

Example 14

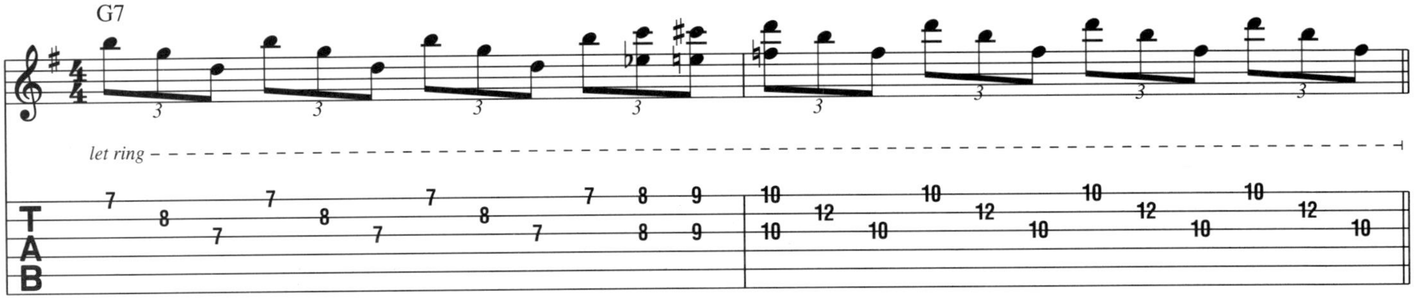

TRACK 15

Example 15

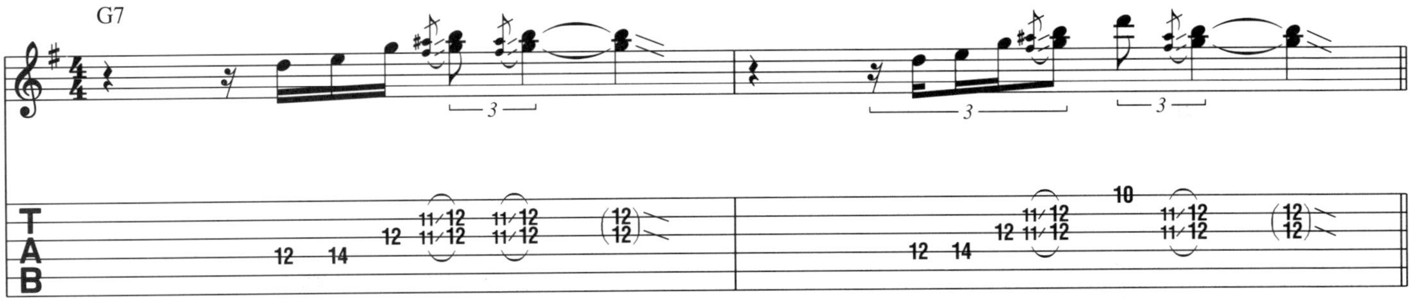

Bars 3 and 4

Here is where you feel the anticipation of that IV chord coming in bar 5. Since it's the I chord for two bars here, you can play G major pentatonic riffs as well as any minor pentatonic riffs. It's also nice to work the two together as Example 24 does. Check out Example 22 for a big S-T-R-E-T-C-H.

TRACK 16

Example 16

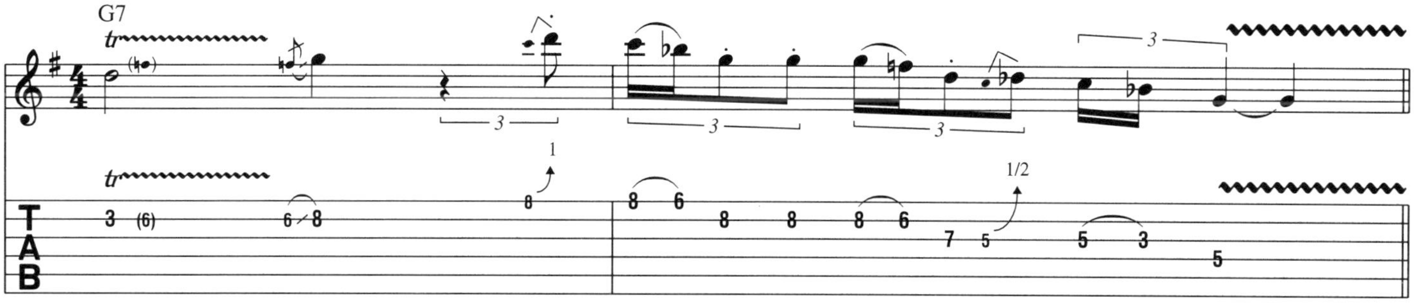

TRACK 17

Example 17

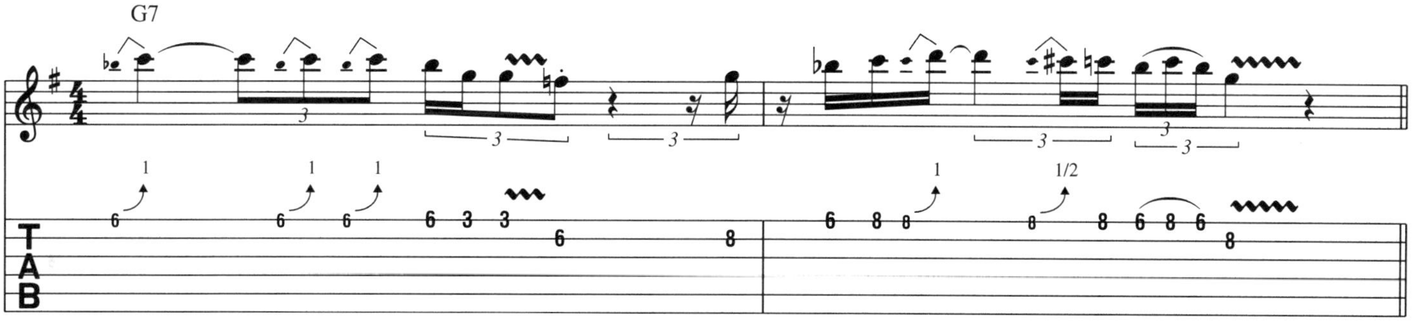

TRACK 18

Example 18

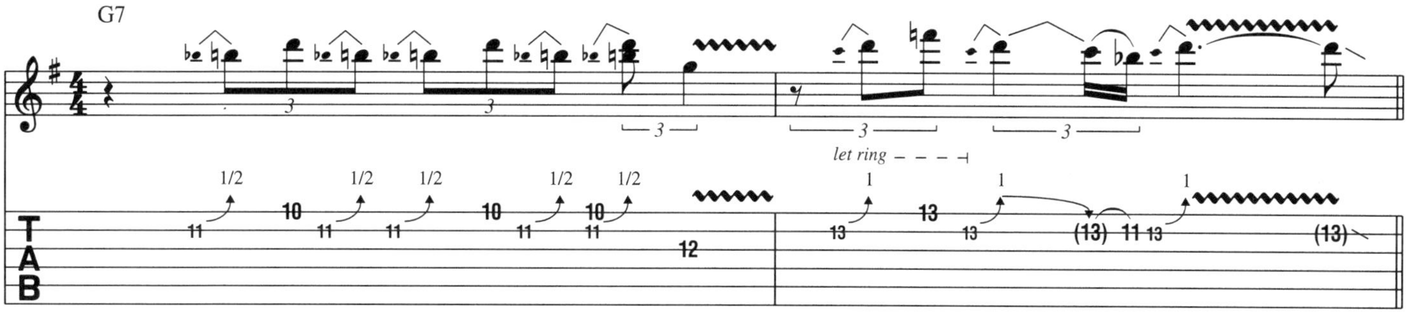

TRACK 19

Example 19

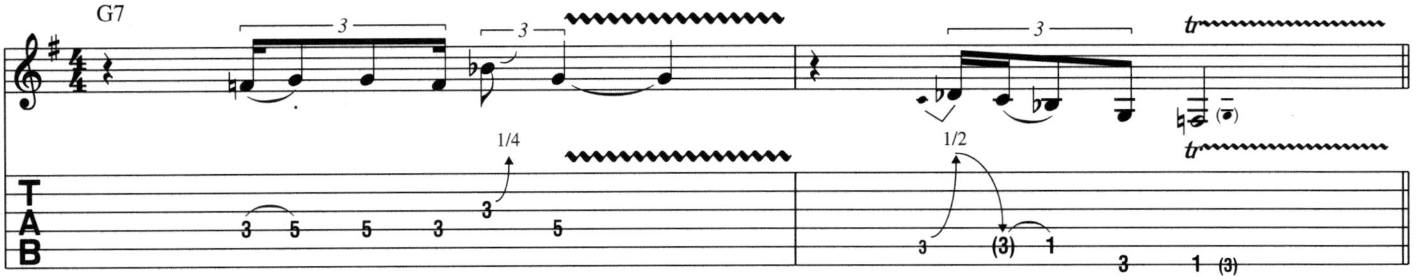

TRACK 20

Example 20

TRACK 21

Example 21

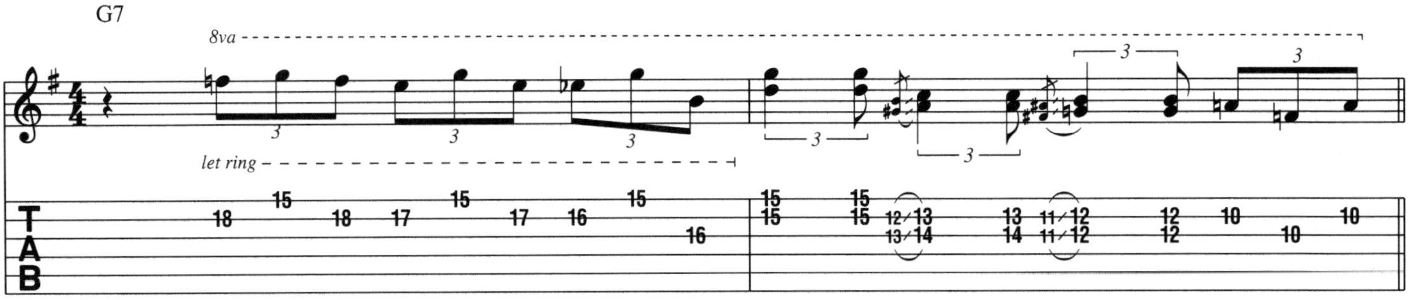

TRACK 22

Example 22

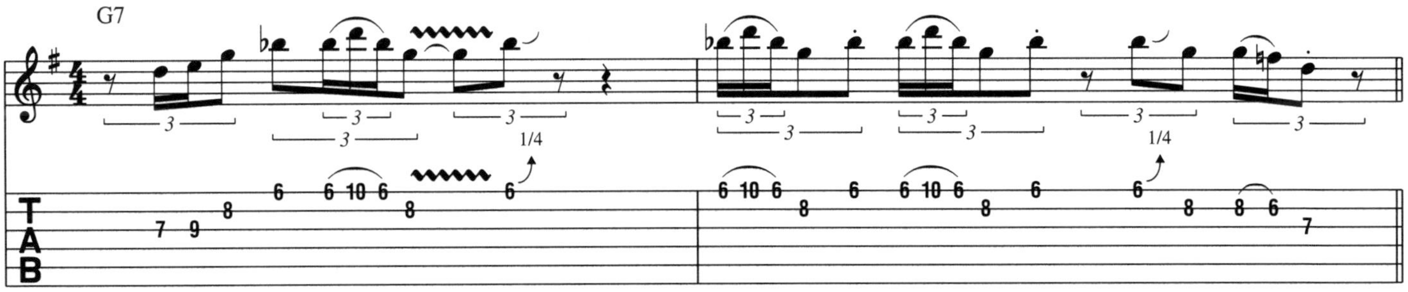

TRACK 23

Example 23

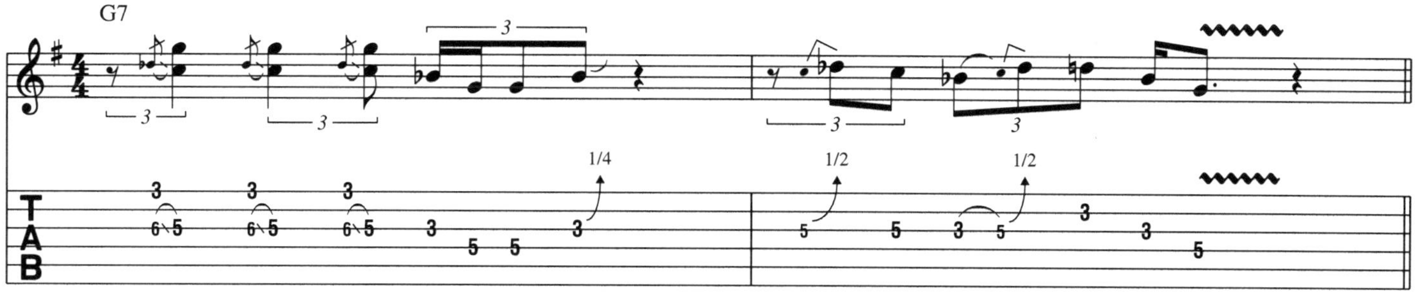

TRACK 24

Example 24

TRACK 25

Example 25

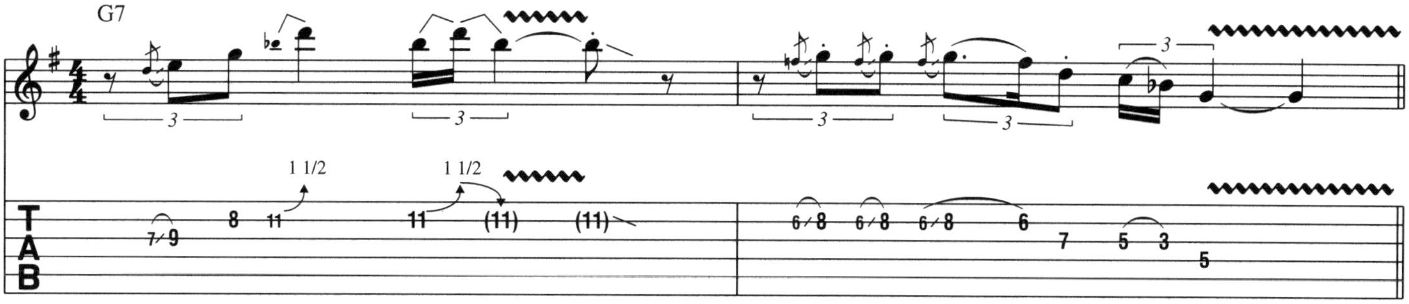

Bars 5 and 6

Here, everything sounds fresh because we have that big chord change. If you play riffs that stay in the G minor pentatonic scale, you can feel them pull against the C chord (IV) to great effect (Examples 27, 28, 30, 33, and 34). You also have the option of moving with the chord change for a different sound (Examples 26, 29, 31, 32, and 35).

TRACK 26

Example 26

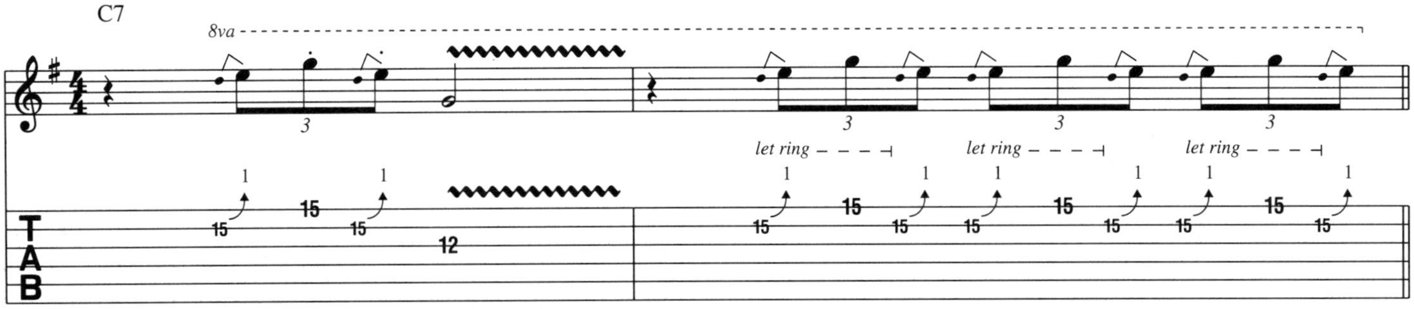

TRACK 27

Example 27

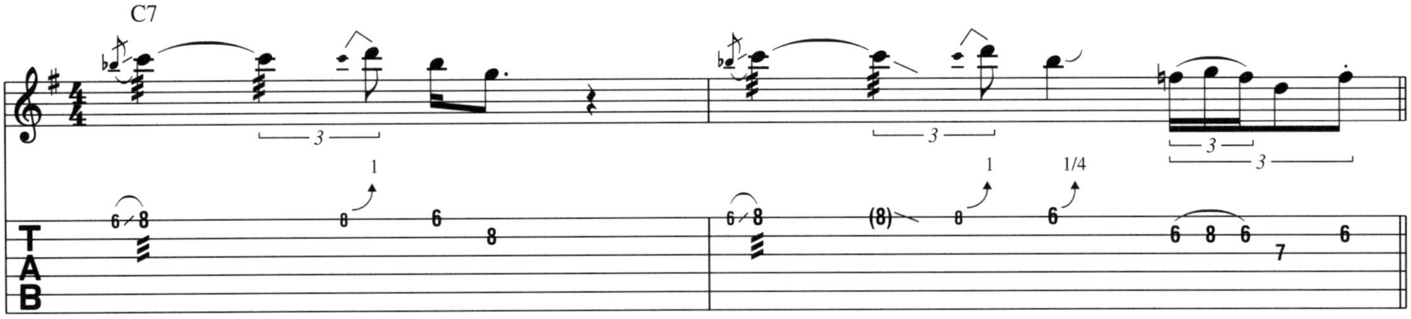

TRACK 28

Example 28

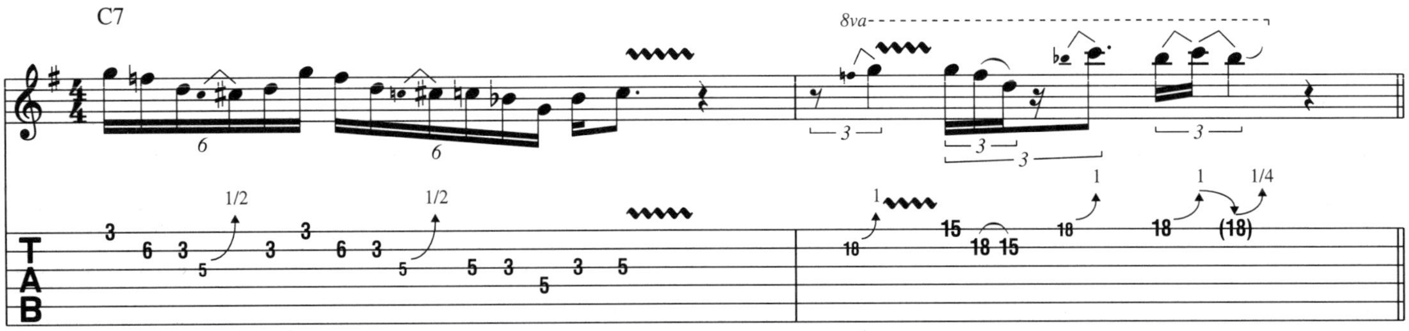

TRACK 29

Example 29

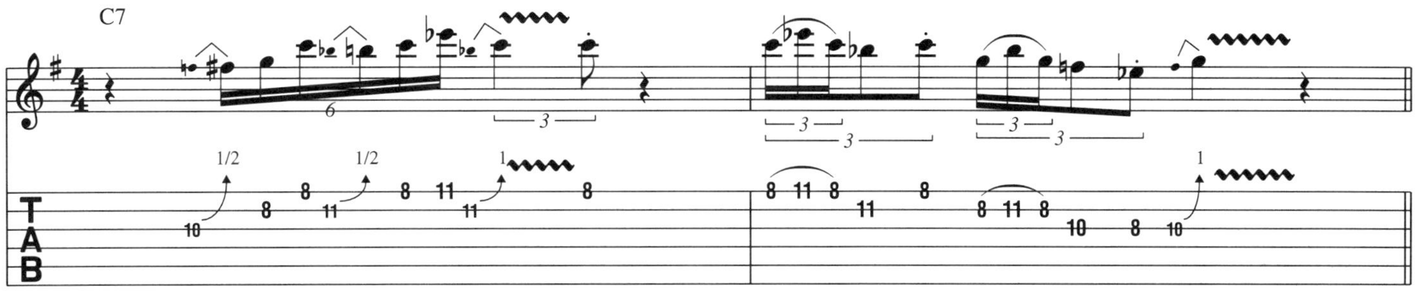

TRACK 30

Example 30

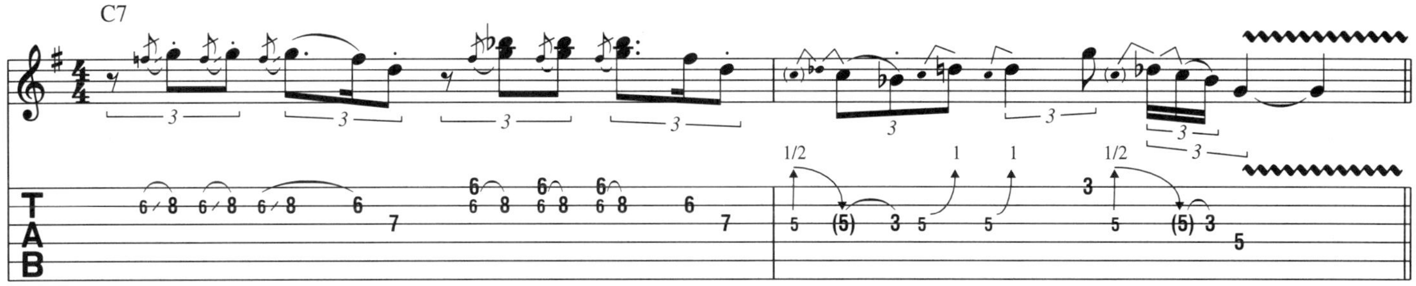

TRACK 31

Example 31

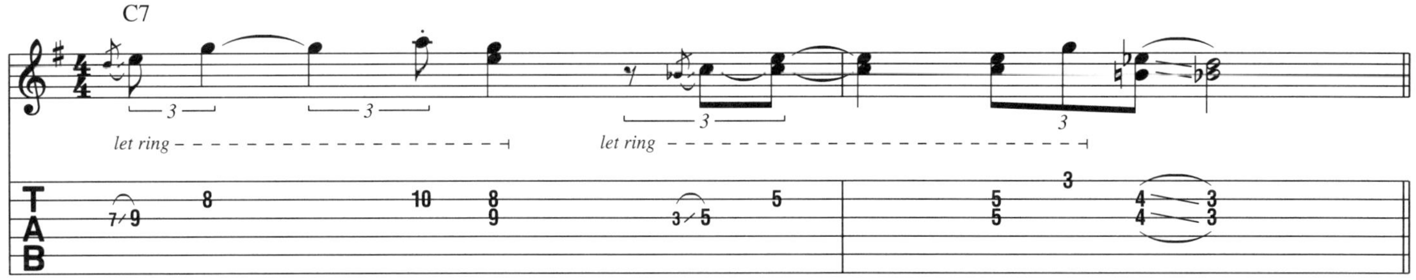

TRACK 32

Example 32

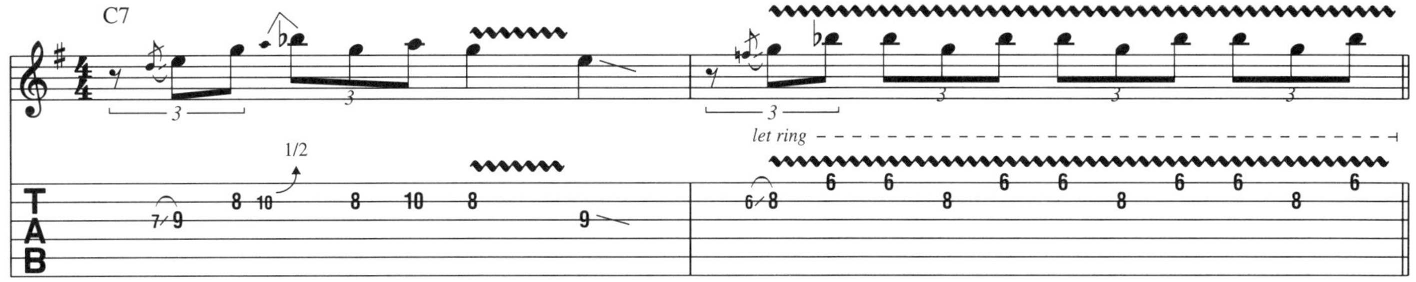

TRACK 33

Example 33

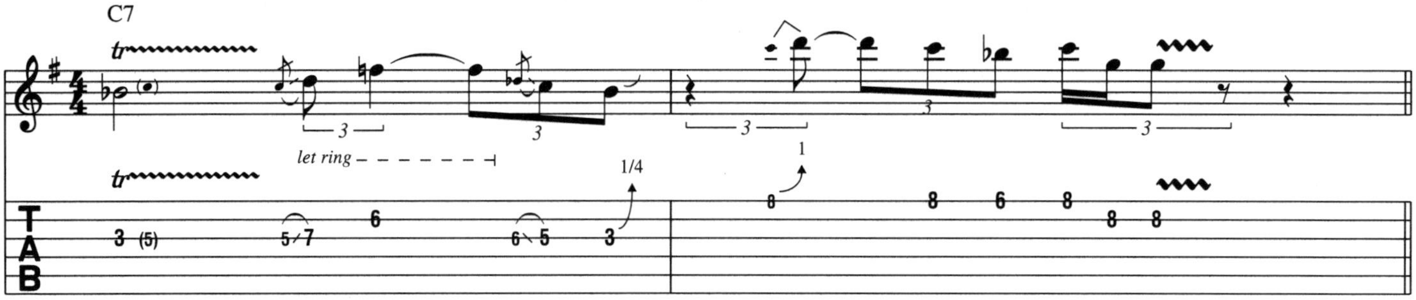

TRACK 34

Example 34

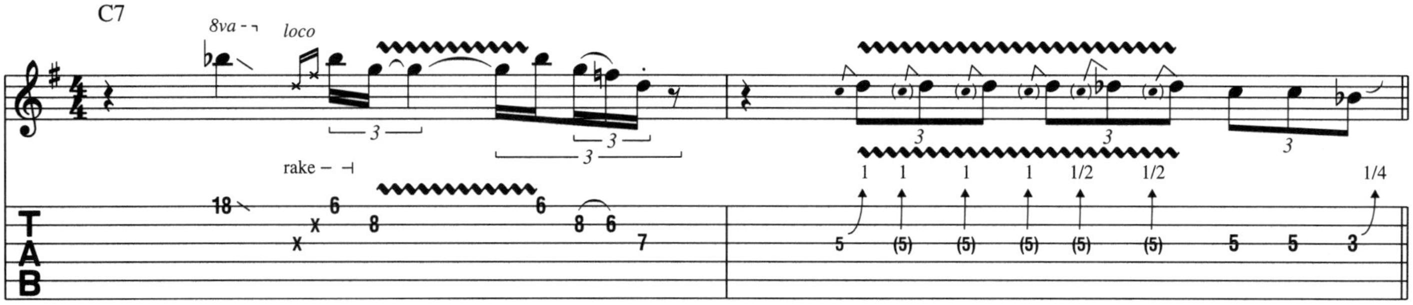

TRACK 35

Example 35

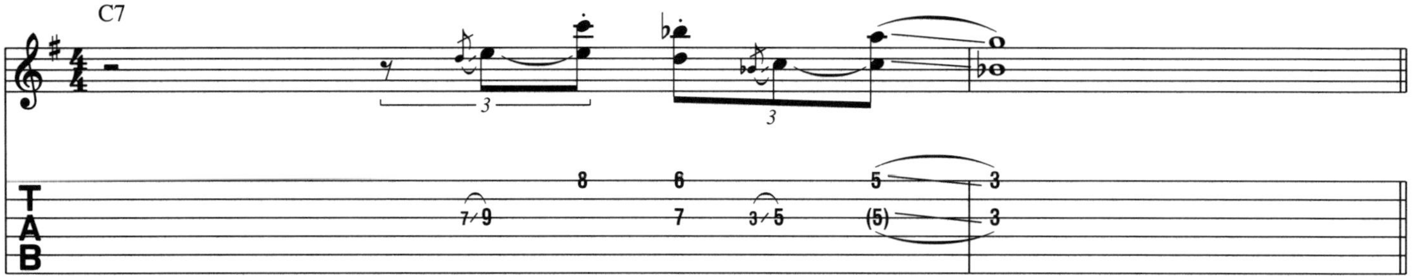

Bars 7 and 8

These two bars function much the same as bars 3 and 4. What they have in common, besides the I chord, is a feeling of momentary stability before the next change. In this case, we are anticipating the V chord. What this means is that most of the riffs for bars 3–4 and bars 7–8 are interchangeable.

TRACK 36

Example 36

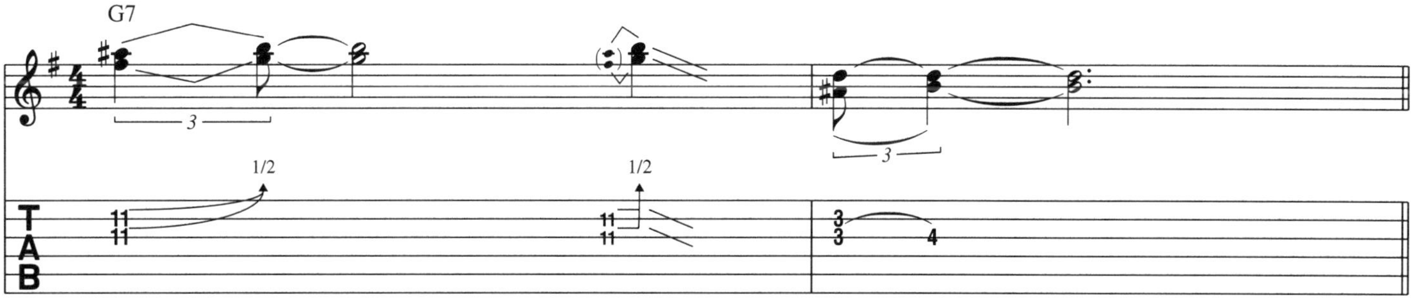

TRACK 37

Example 37

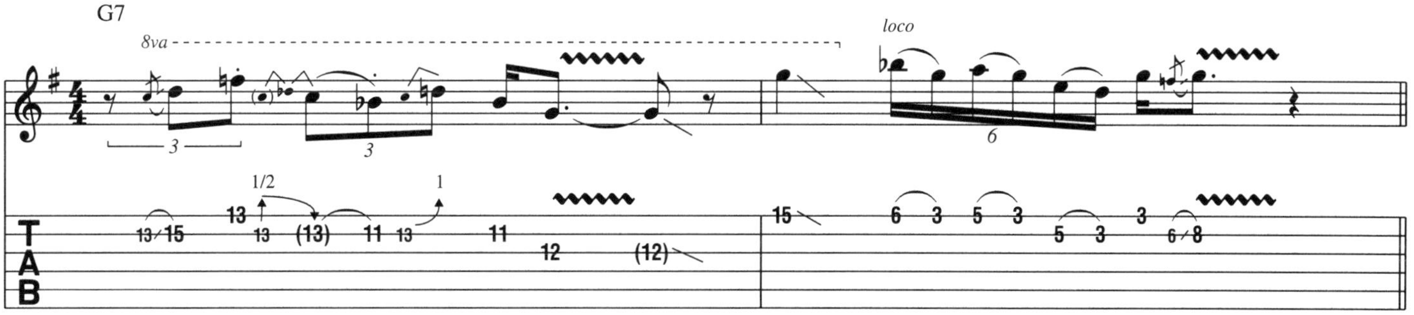

TRACK 38

Example 38

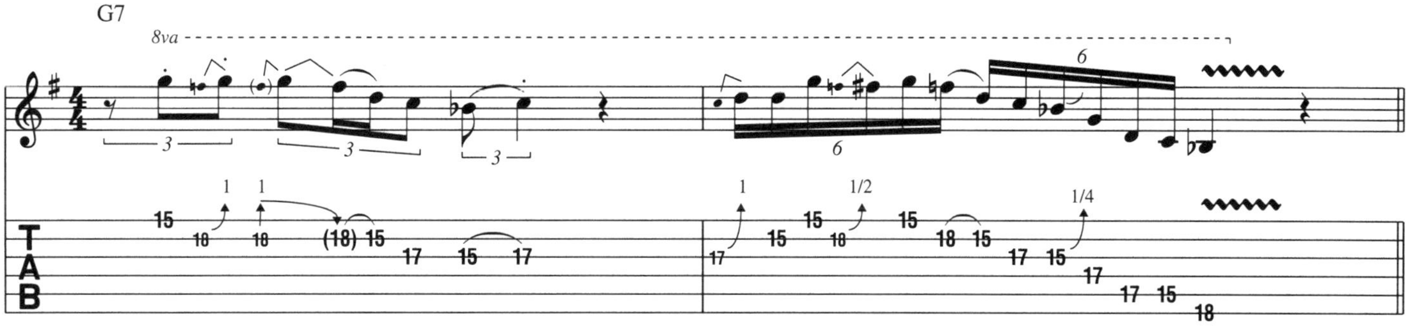

TRACK 39

Example 39

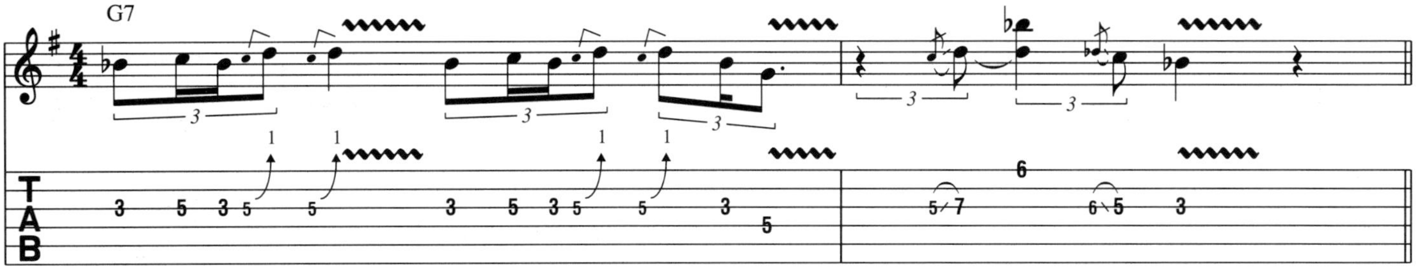

TRACK 40

Example 40

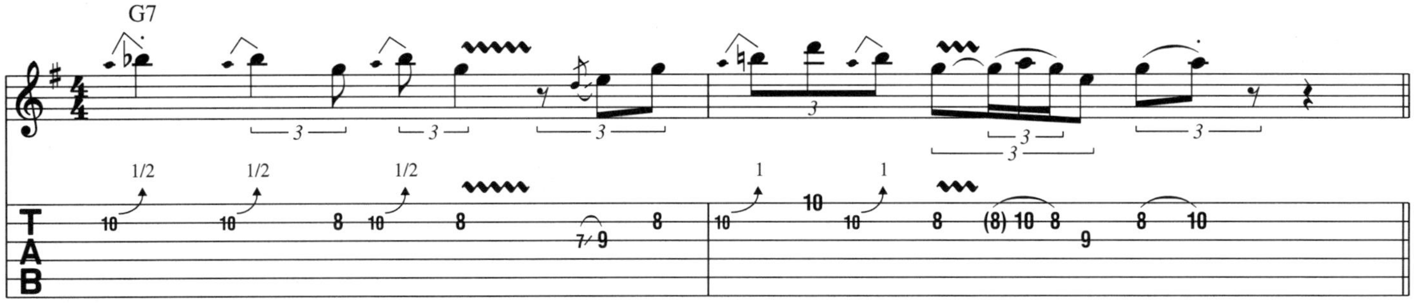

TRACK 41

Example 41

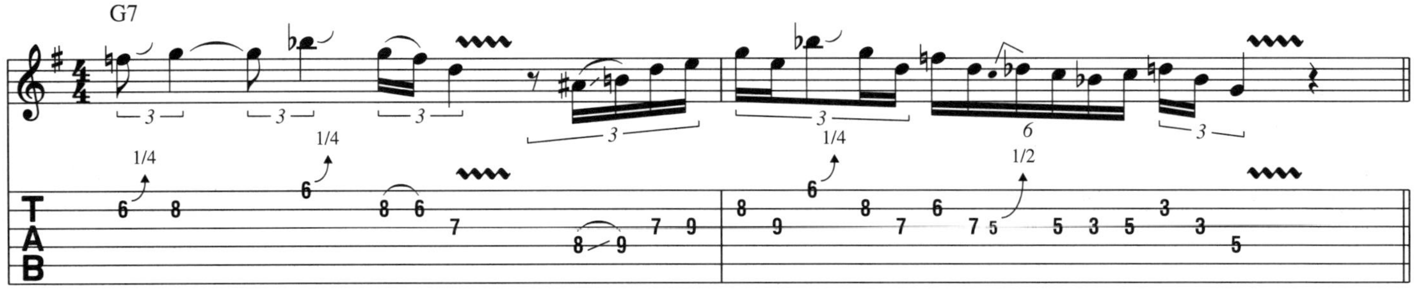

TRACK 42

Example 42

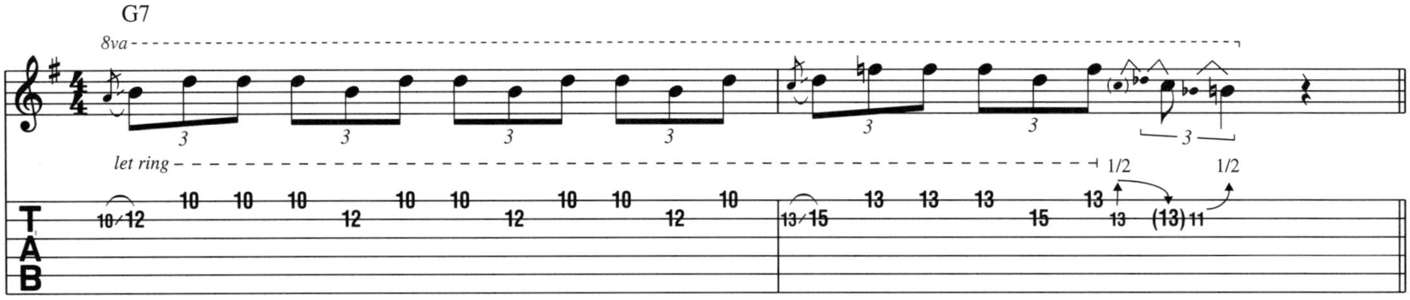

Example 43

TRACK 43

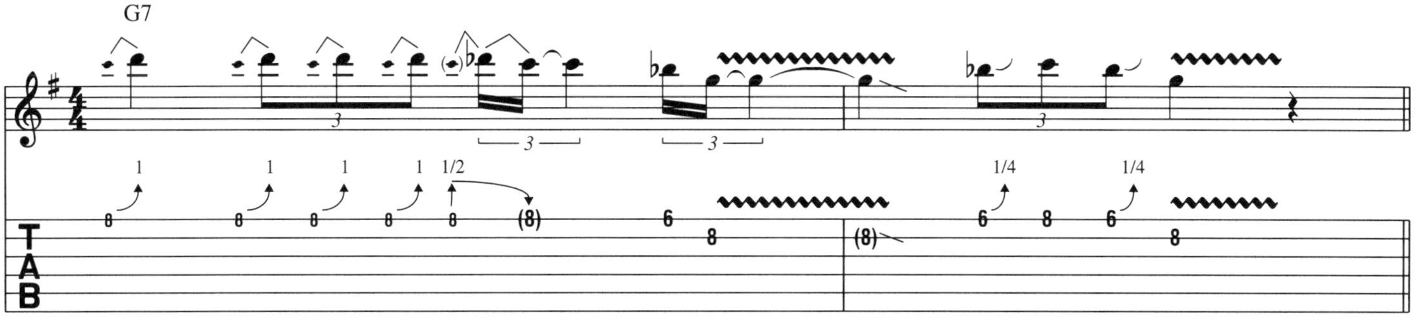

Example 44

TRACK 44

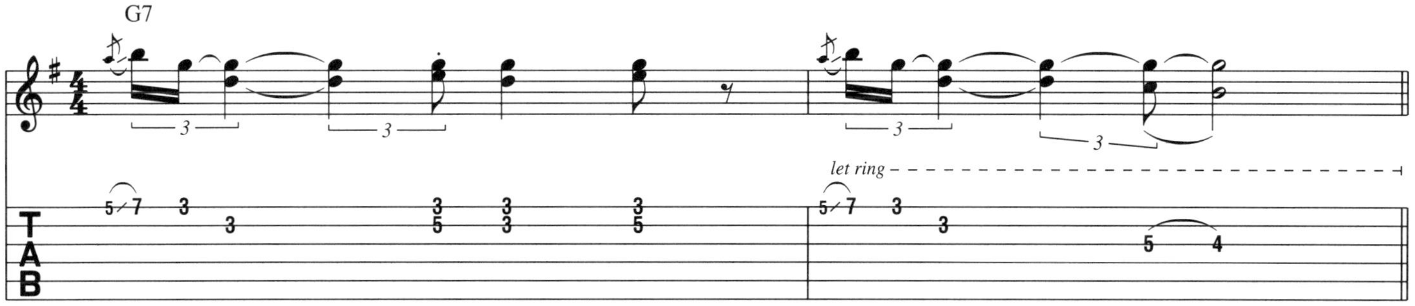

Example 45

TRACK 45

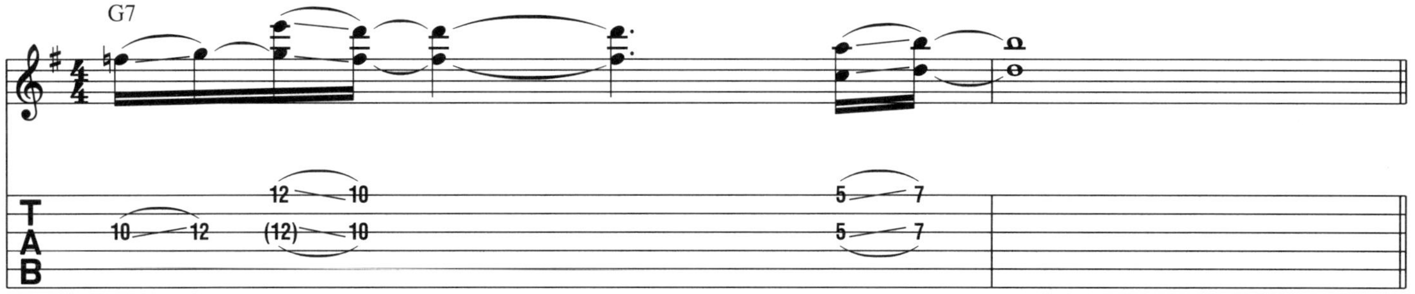

Bars 9 and 10

The last four bars of the blues is the big payoff. It all begins here with the V chord descending into the IV chord. You can modulate with these changes (Examples 48, 51, 54, and 55) or accentuate the tension of letting the G minor pentatonic riffs pull against them (Examples 46, 47, 49, and 50).

TRACK 46

Example 46

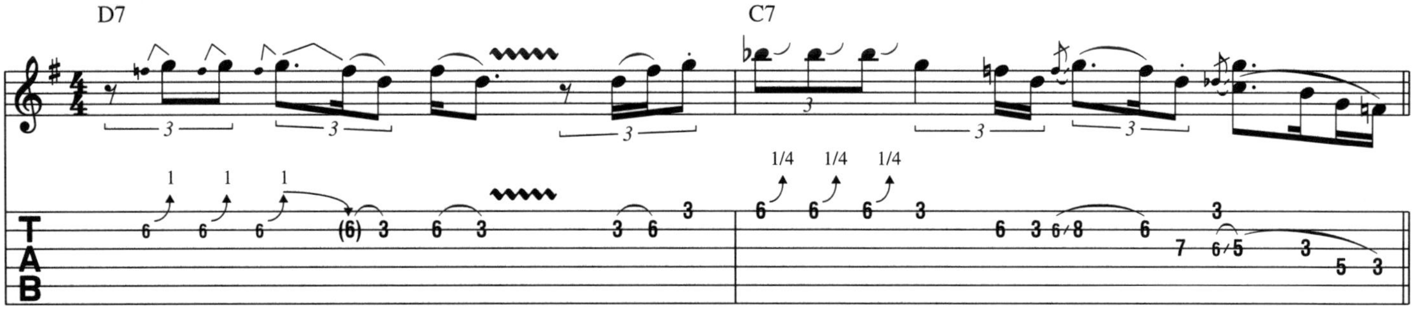

TRACK 47

Example 47

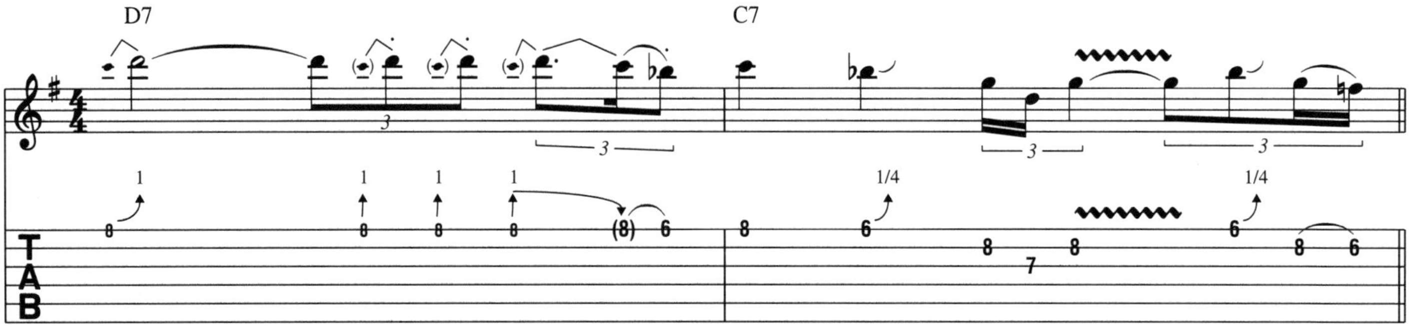

TRACK 48

Example 48

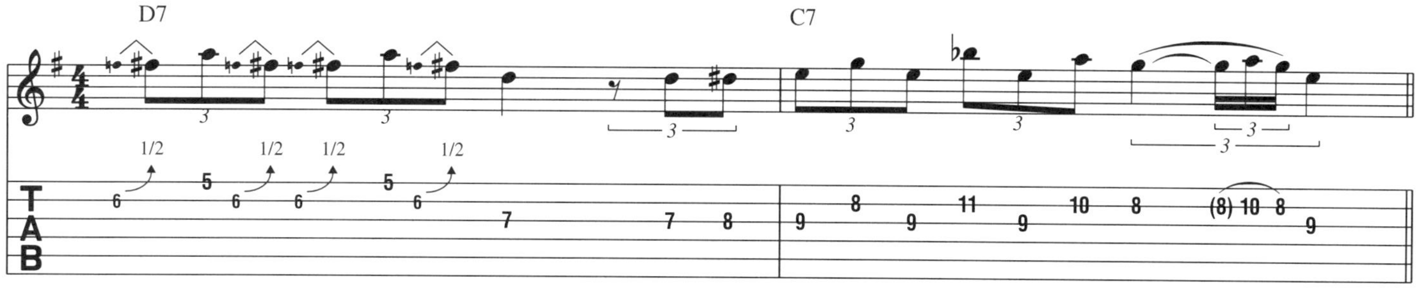

TRACK 49

Example 49

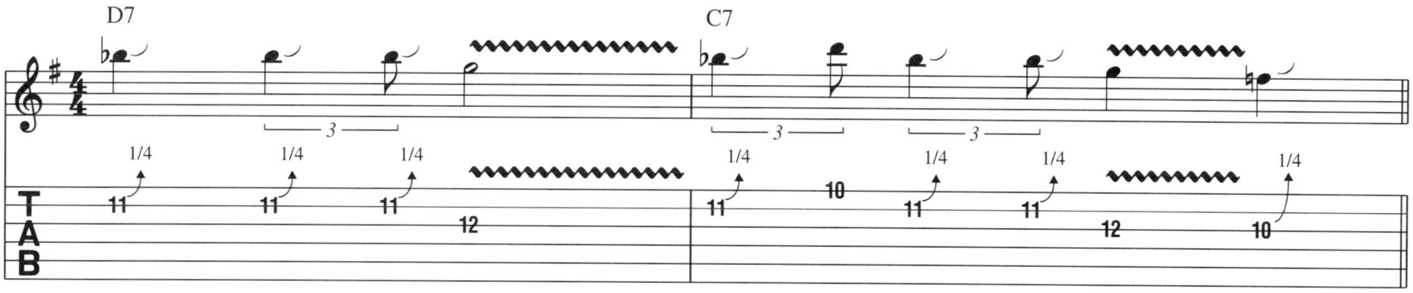

TRACK 50

Example 50

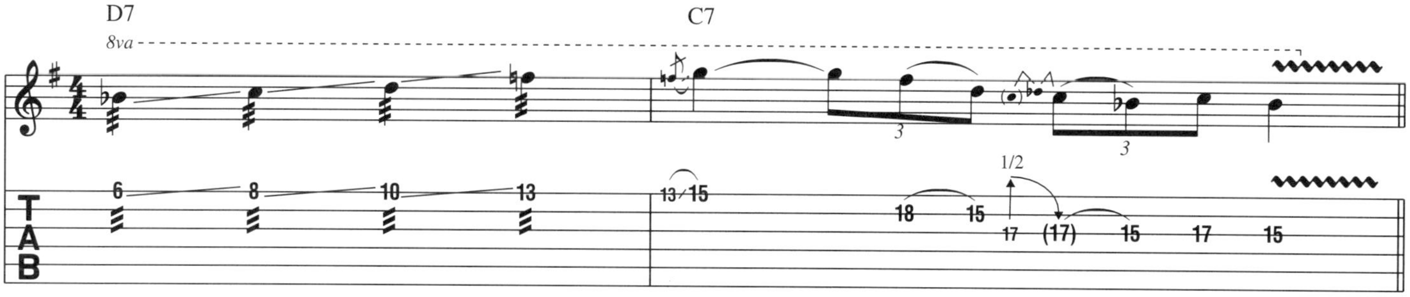

TRACK 51

Example 51

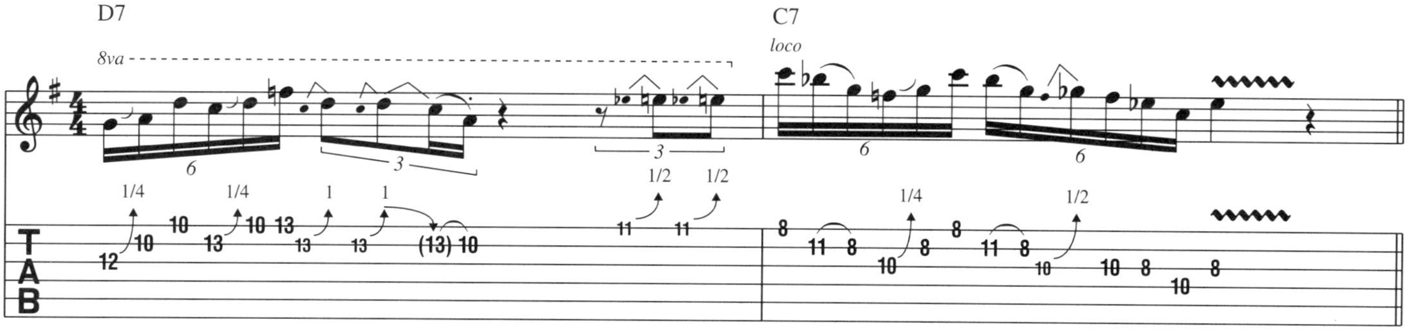

TRACK 52

Example 52

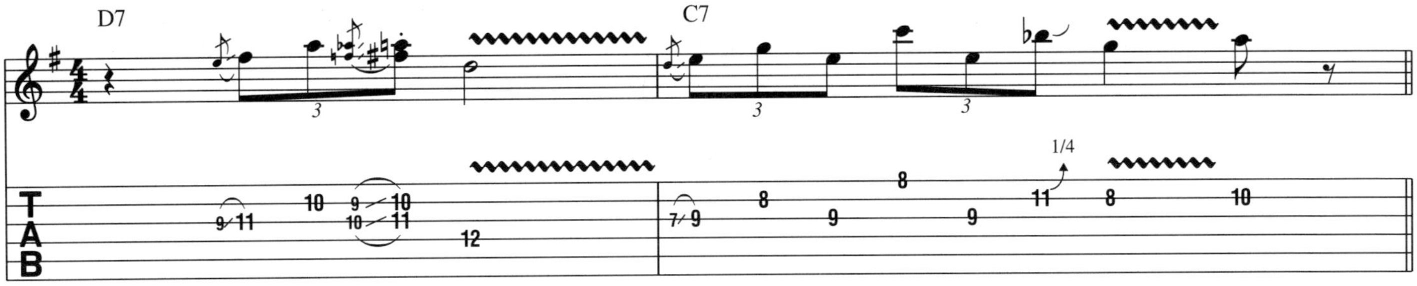

TRACK 53

Example 53

TRACK 54

Example 54

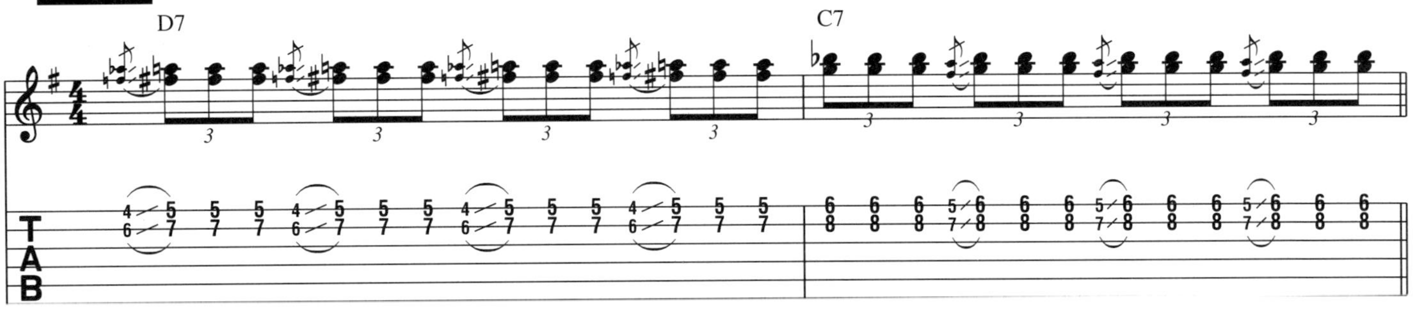

TRACK 55

Example 55

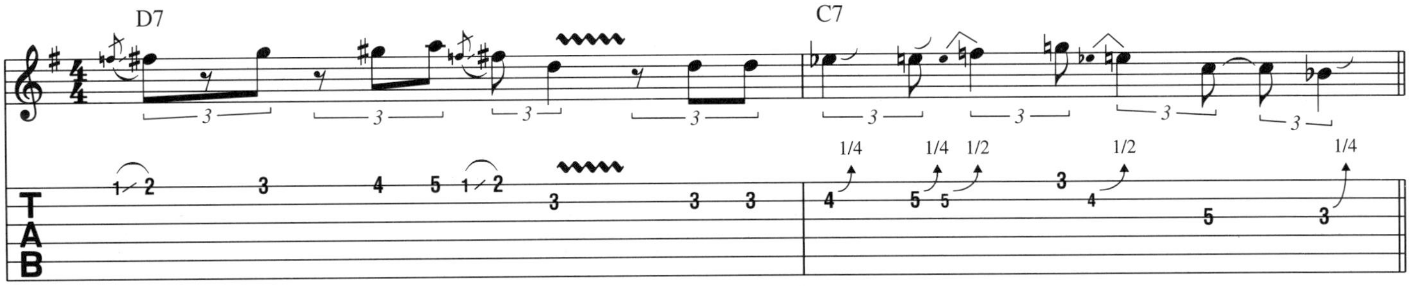

Bars 11 and 12

These last two bars are the turnaround. As the name implies, its function is to take us back to the top; this can be accomplished in any number of ways. The turnaround featured here is called the "I–IV–I–V." This is very popular because of its great root motion and the feeling of a "restatement" of the previous ten bars. The riffs below will work with just about any turnaround you'll encounter. Later, you'll get the chance to play them with another common turnaround, the I–V.

TRACK 56

Example 56

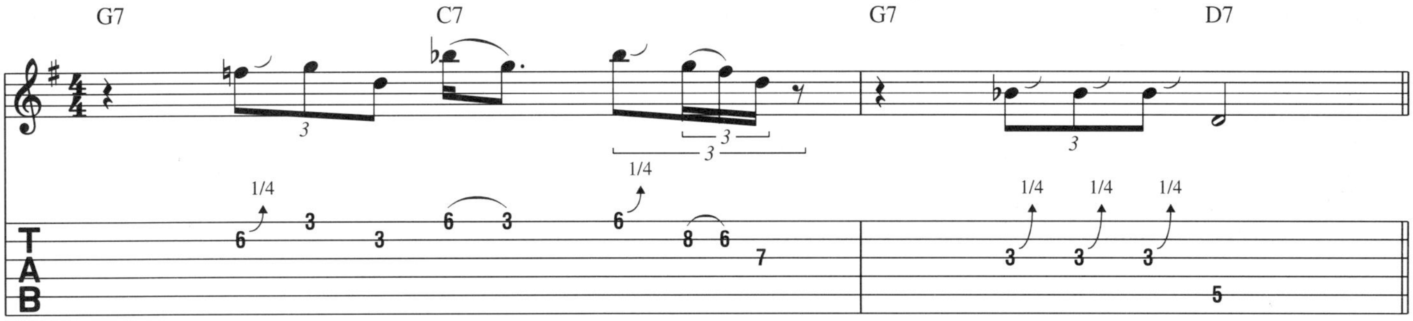

TRACK 57

Example 57

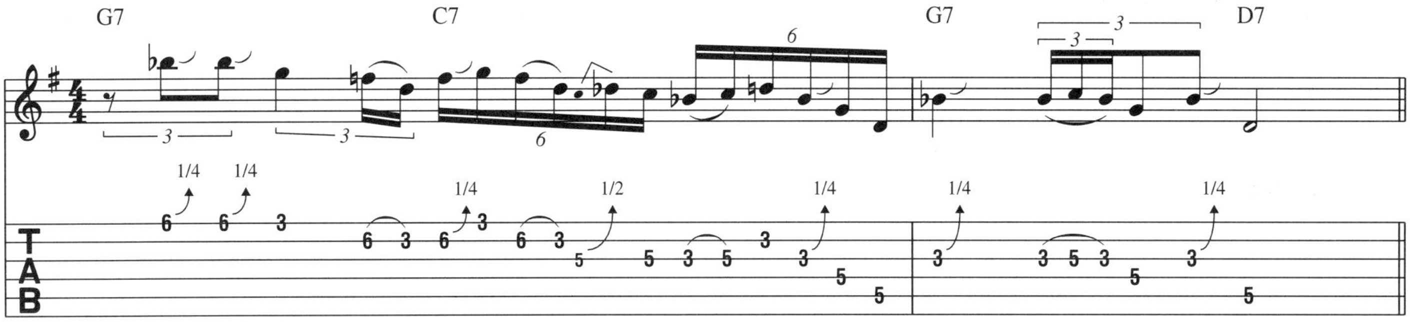

TRACK 58

Example 58

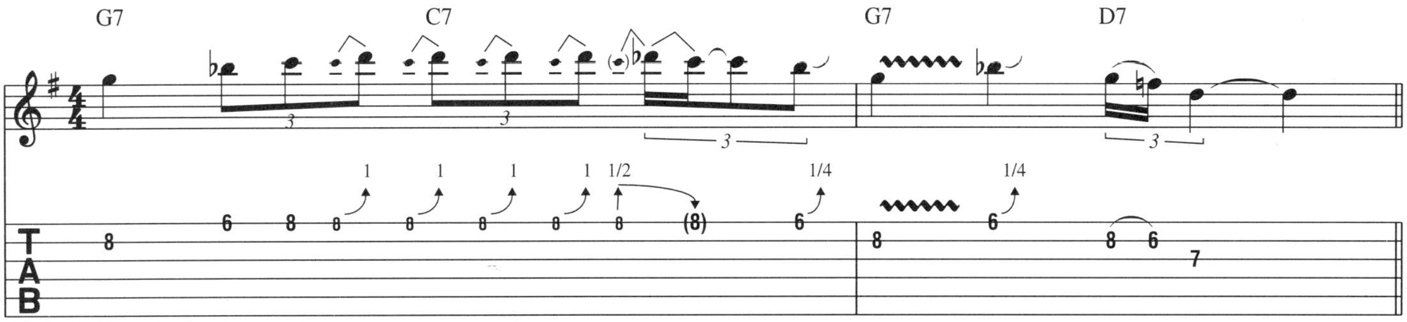

TRACK 59

Example 59

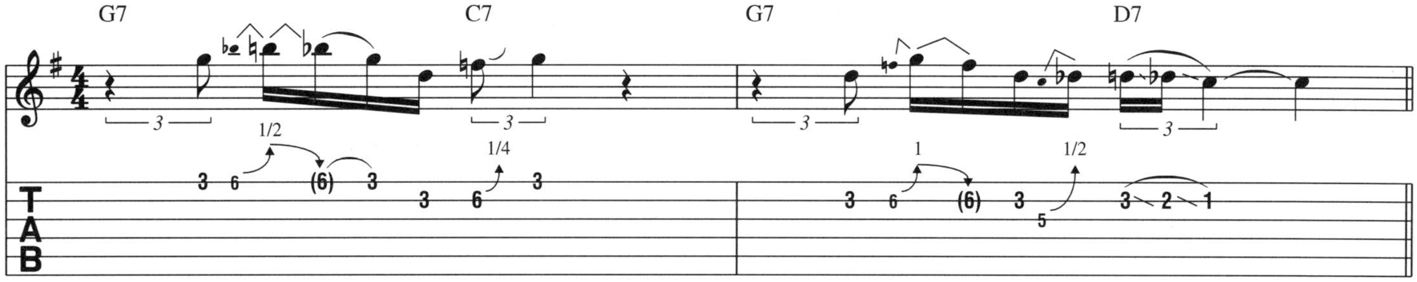

TRACK 60

Example 60

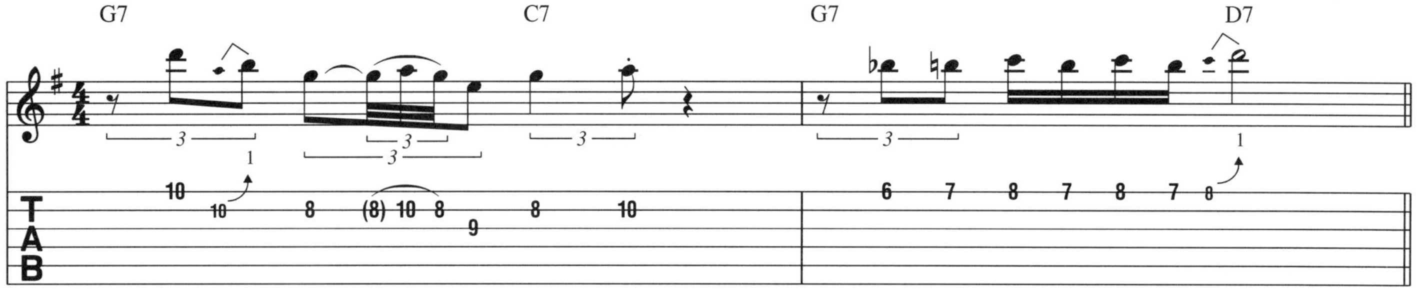

TRACK 61

Example 61

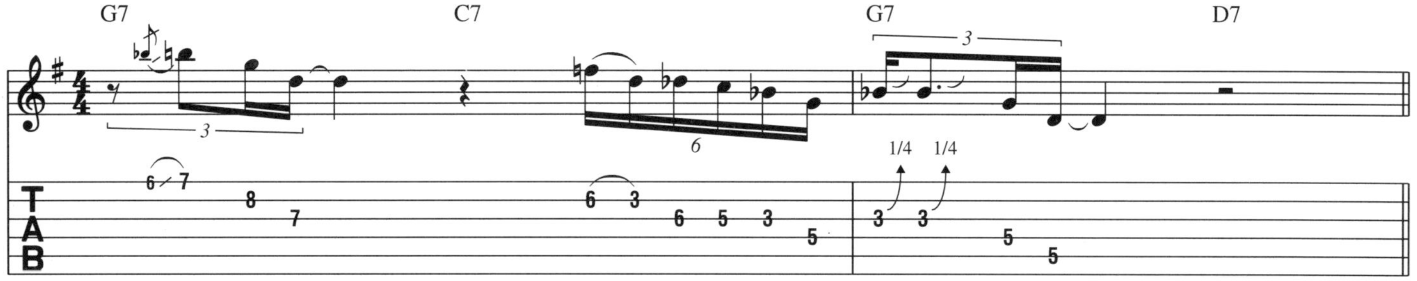

TRACK 62

Example 62

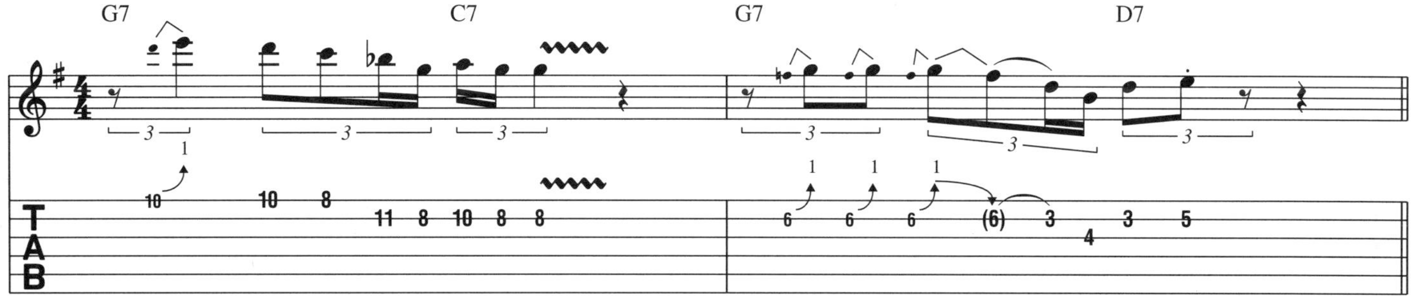

TRACK 63

Example 63

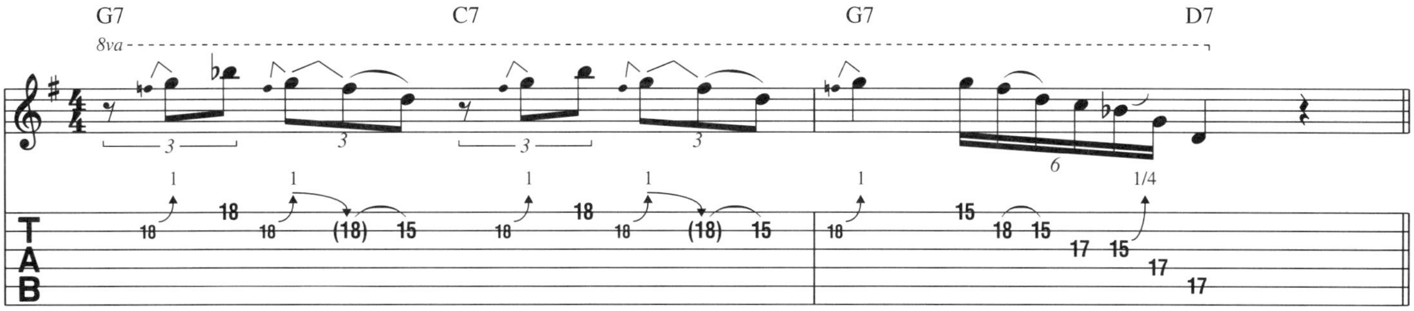

TRACK 64

Example 64

TRACK 65

Example 65

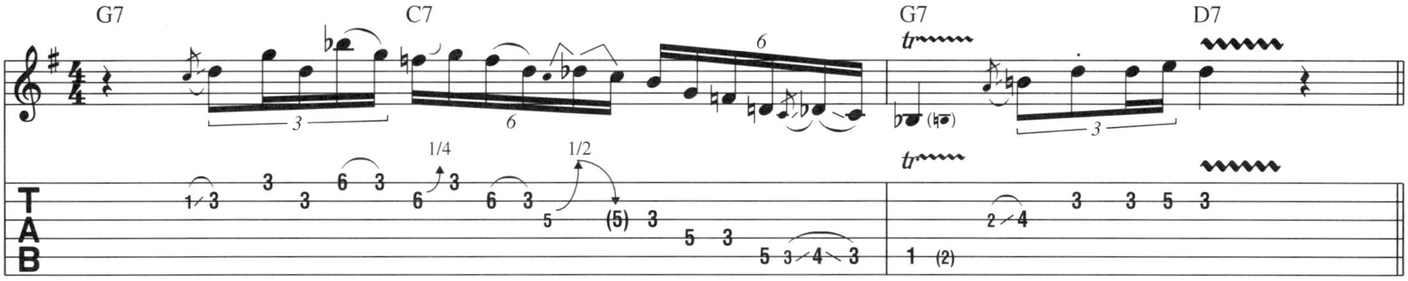

TRACK 66

Example 66

TRACK 67

Example 67

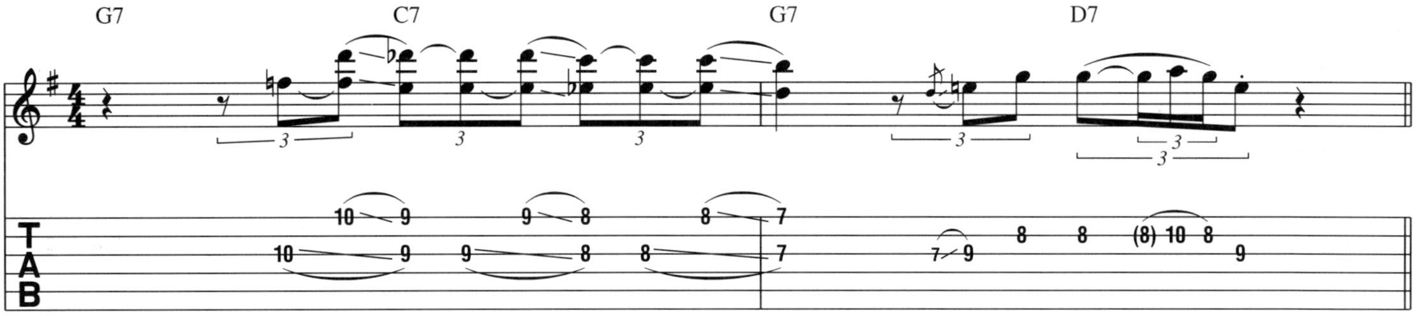

TRACK 68

Example 68

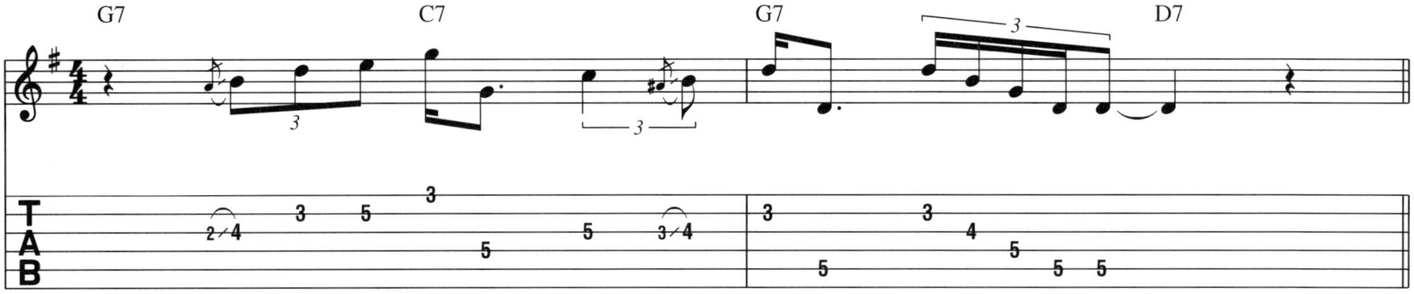

TRACK 69

Example 69

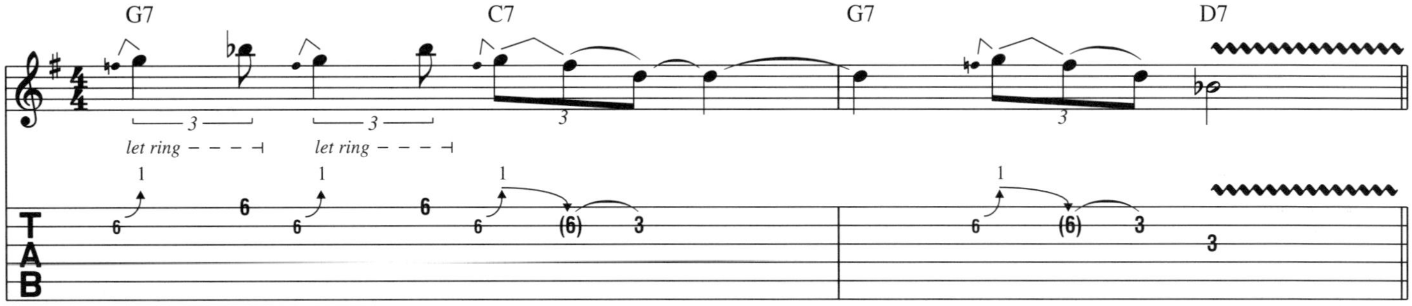

The riff below works solely with the I–IV–I–V turnaround, since it outlines those changes.

TRACK 70

Example 70

Complete Solos

Here are two complete solos. The first is the "template" we've been using throughout this book. The second features the "slow four" combined with the I–V turnaround.

TRACK 71

Example 71: Solo 1

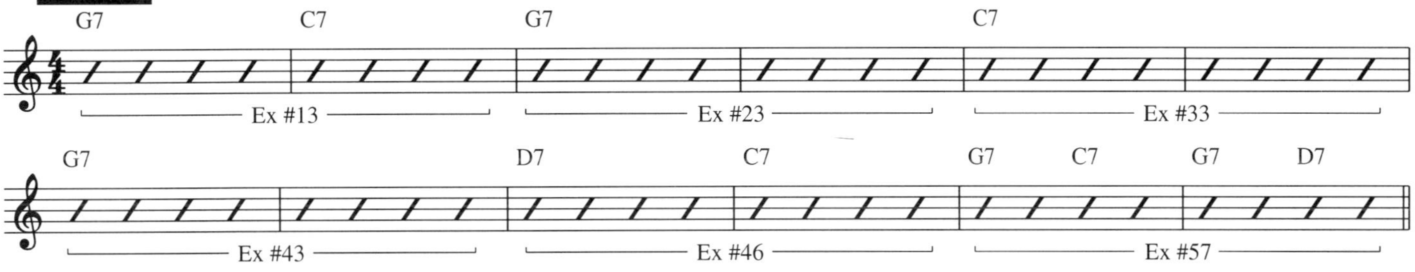

TRACK 72

Example 72: Solo 2

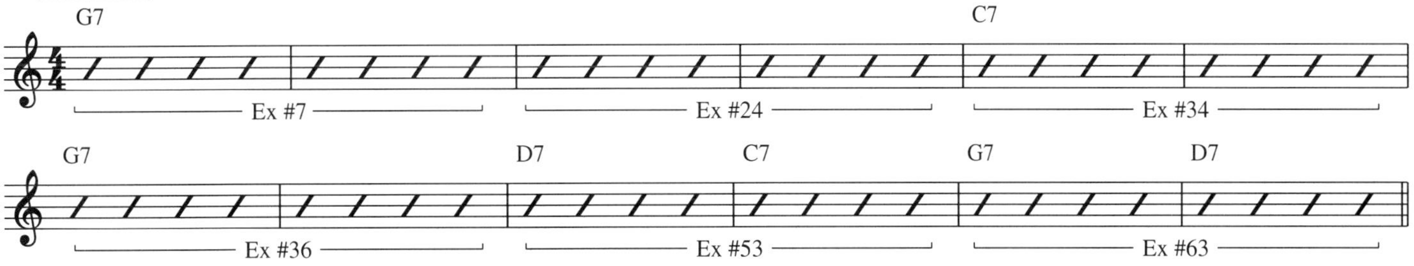

Music Minus Me

Now it's your turn to solo. For each key you'll get a chance to play with two different versions.

TRACK 73

Example 73: Music Minus Me 1

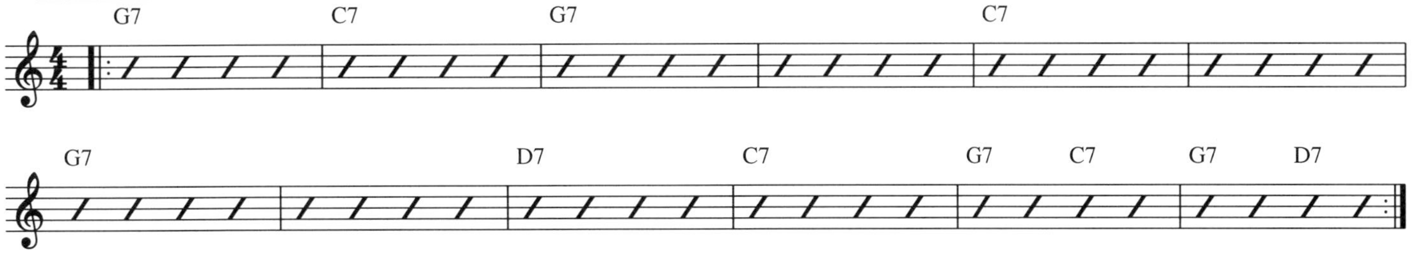

TRACK 74

Example 74: Music Minus Me 2

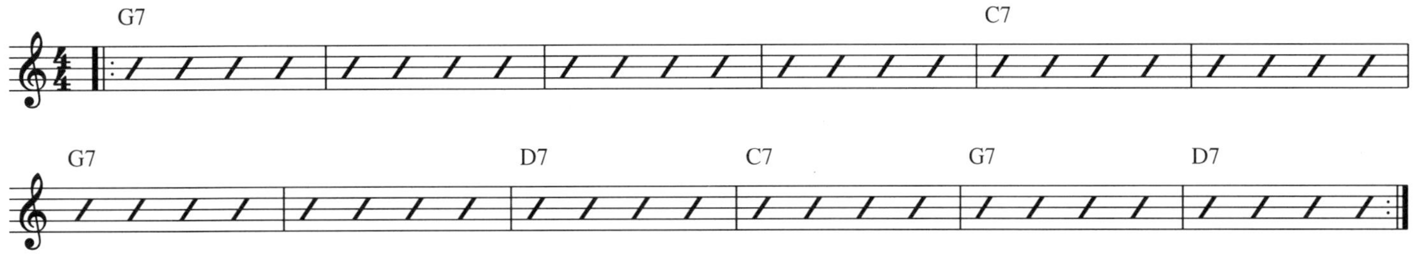

Example 75: Music Minus Me 3

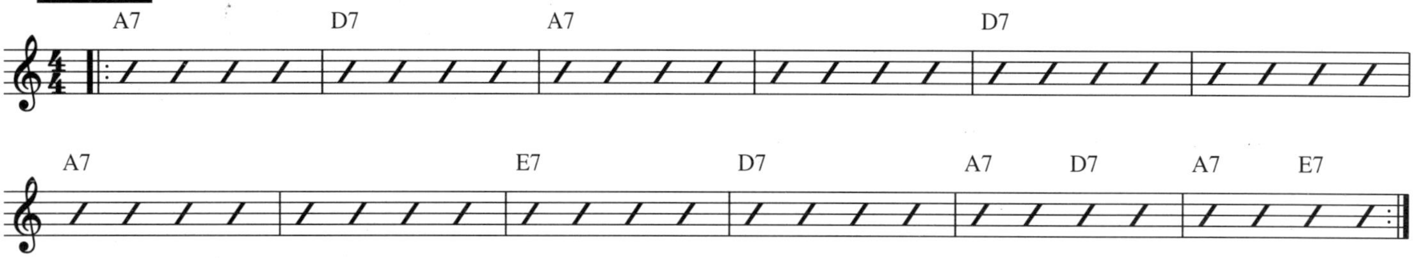

Example 76: Music Minus Me 4

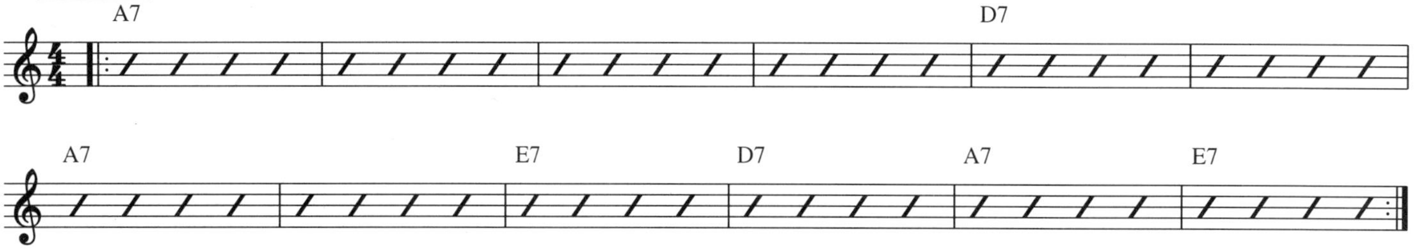

Example 77: Music Minus Me 5

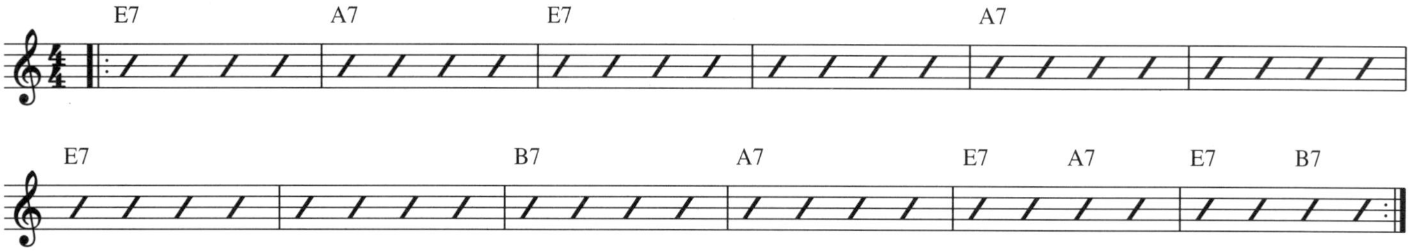

Example 78: Music Minus Me 6

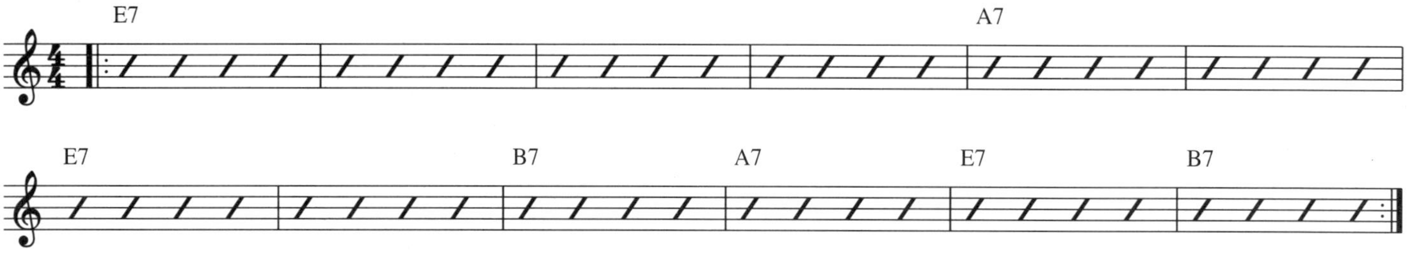

Afterword

When you feel comfortable with all of the riffs in this book, try playing them in different blues contexts. Also, experiment with shifting the riffs to different starting points. You'll find that an infinite number of possibilities will present themselves.

I hope this book has given you a good foundation of riffs from which to choose when playing your own blues solos. Never stop experimenting—and keep jamming!